CW00600906

MILLION MAKERS

All net proceeds donated to The Prince's Trust (registered charity no.1079675)

A Little Taste of Yorkshire

First paperback edition printed 2014 in the United Kingdom

First paperback edition printed 2014 in the United Kingdom

ISBN 978-0-9931165-0-6

Published by Hallmark EDP
Copyright holder Hallmark EDP
For more copies of this book, please email: Million_Makers@hallmark-uk.com

Designed and Set by : Hallmark Million Makers

Printed in Great Britain by:
Bist Media
4 Fairfax House
Cottingley Business Park
Bingley
West Yorkshire
BD22 8JX
Email:media@bist.co.uk

CONTENTS

The Magpie Café - Cullen Skink Whitby Style 13

Crafthouse & Angelica - Roast Cod Fillet 17

Forster's Bistro & Deli - Tuna Steaks with Salsa 21

Tharavadu - Kerala Fish Curry 25

Cerutti's - Yorkshire Lemon Sole & Crab 29

The Yorkshire Meatball Co. - Lamb & Cranberry Balls 33

THE 1875 - Goan Pork Vinho De Alho 37

Gimbals - Slow Braised Brisket of Beef & Rock Rhubarb Cocktail 41

The Cleveland Tontine - Hare Trio 45

Le Cochon Aveugle - Brined Chicken 49

Don't Tell Titus - Rustic Beans Cassoulet 53

El-Piano - Mexi Trio 57

Pipe & Glass Inn - Yorkshire Rhubarb Trifle 61

Towngate Brasserie - Millionaire Shortbread 65

Trenchers - Fish Pie 69

The Old Vicarage - Roast Fillet of Cod 71

Hansa's - Shrikhand 75

Le Box Bistro - Sticky Toffee Pudding 77

Relish - Wholegrain Mustard & Cheese Sausage Rolls 81

Eat Me Café - Seagull Pie (don't worry it's not seagulls!) 83

Primo's - Pulled Pork Sandwich 85

Bean Loved - Cafetiere & The Perfect Poached Eggs 87

Crumbs Cupcakery - Crème Egg Cupcakes 91

Lakeside Café - Maple & Pecan Triangles 95

Filmore & Union - Chicken Tagine with Dates & Honey 99

Krave - Huevos Rancheros (Ranchers Eggs) 101

Shibden Inn - Salad of Calderdale Cheese Bon Bons 107

Bundobust - Onion Gobi Bhaji-onion, Cauliflower & Spinach Bhajis 111

The Devonshire Arms - Beetroot Cured Salmon 113

Aston Springs Farm - Astons Ultimate Burger 119

Keelham Farm Shop - Yorkshire Tapas 123

Blacker Hall Farm - Beef & Chorizo Casserole 127

Farmer Copleys - Venison & Beetroot Burger 129

Belgrave Music Hall - Fu-Schnikens 135

Pho (Trinity Kitchen) - Pho Ga (Chicken Noodle Soup) 139

Rola Wala - Mark & Danny's Epic Breakfast Naan Roll Flip 143

Cobble Kitchen - Raspberry & Almond Cake 147

I Love Cheesecake - Chocolate Cheesecake Brownie 151

El Kantina - Ninja Nachos 155

My Organic Home - Organic Triple Toffee Cake 159

Yorkshire Pudd - Roast Beef, Yorkshire Pudding & Gravy 161

Curry Cuisine Cookery School - Chicken Masala 165

Shepherds Purse Artisan Cheeses - Harrogate Blue Cheese Mash 167

Vincents - Espresso Hazelnut Brownies 171

Busy Bees - Bienenstich (Bee Sting Cake) 173

Boxpizza - Grilled Chicken Florentine Pizza 175

The Tasty Teams Recipes 179

Our Lovely Sponsors 195

THE → TEAM

A Little Taste of Yorkshire was put together as part of The Prince's Trust Million Makers challenge. The Million Makers challenge is an entrepreneurial fundraising competition, which sees talented teams from companies across the UK attempt to raise in excess of £10,000 for The Prince's Trust.

We are the Hallmark Million Makers! Based in Bradford, we are passionate about Yorkshire and about everything this great county has to offer. We have created this book to showcase independent businesses across the region and to provide a unique collection of recipes from Yorkshire people in the know. We are also hoping to raise lots of money too! We are Beth, Lois, Jackie, Katie C, Katie W, Joel and Zully and we hope that you enjoy using this cookbook as much as we have enjoyed creating it, and that together we can raise as much money as possible for The Prince's Trust.

BIG
THANK YOU'S

- To all of those lovely colleagues at Hallmark who have helped make this cookbook a huge success
- An extra special thanks to the creative and editorial team at Hallmark, especially Kelly Wykman, for working her creative magic
- To our mentors, coaches and managers who have supported us on this journey
- Bist Media for their local printing skills
- All you lovely local businesses and sponsors who have donated recipes, time and money!
- And a massive thanks to you for buying the book and supporting The Prince's Trust. We hope you enjoy!

MILLION MAKERS

All net proceeds donated to The Prince's Trust (registered charity no.1079675)

The Prince's Trust supports disadvantaged young people aged 13 to 30 by giving practical and financial support to those who need it most. They help young people who are long term unemployed, those who have struggled at school, offenders and ex-offenders and those who have been through the care system. Through a range of tailored programmes, they help individuals to overcome personal barriers and develop key skills, confidence and motivation,enabling them to move into work, education or training. The Prince's Trust will help 58,000 disadvantaged young people this year and to do this need to raise almost £1 million a week.

Laura Craddock

Joshua Brockbank

Alex Gray

Stefan Schiefer

Joshua Brockbank

STAITHES LSP

Stefan Schiefer

Pen

dale 1¼ ml

Pennine Way

Joshua Brockbank

Joshua Brock

Joshua Brockbank

Stefan Schiefer

Alex Gray

Stefan Schiefer

WHY YORKSHIRE?

- Yorkshire is the largest county in the UK.

- It's called 'God's Own County'...and with good reason!

- It's home to over 80 Real Ale pubs and breweries, producing almost a third of the UK's beer.

- Yorkshire outperformed in the 2012 Olympics, placing it twelfth in the medal table if regarded as an independent country.

- The most Michelin-Starred restaurants outside of London are in...you've guessed it...Yorkshire!

- Lonely Planet voted Yorkshire as the third best place to visit in the world.

- Yorkshire hosted the Grande Depart of the Tour de France, raising awareness and positive press about how truly great the county is.

- There's a real sense of pride amongst Yorkshire folk and it's got a lot to do with the strength of local produce and eateries!

- Yorkshire's cultural diversity means there's a huge choice of cuisine to explore, from Mexican and Lebanese, through Asian, French and Persian, to Thai, Vietnamese, Italian and Chinese(the list goes on and on...and on!)

All photos taken by Yorkshire photographers: Joshua Brockbank (badgerbank@icloud.com), Stefan Schiefer (www.stefanschiefer.co.uk), Alex Gray (albgray.tumblr.com) and Laura Craddock.

RESTAURANTS

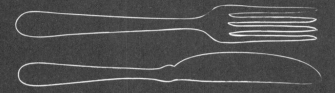

Yorkshire is one of the best regions in the country for food lovers.

It has no less than six Michelin-starred establishments (including my own!) - that's more than any other county in the UK outside London. It also has a huge array of other excellent restaurants, cafes, bars, pubs and street food stalls.

Our produce is second to none. In Yorkshire we do meat, game, fish, cheese, fruit, veg and grains, and our varied landscape, from dramatic coastal locations to rolling pastoral countryside, means we do it all very well.

This 'little taste' of Yorkshire will introduce you to some of the county's best producers and chefs. I hope you enjoy it.

James Mackenzie
Chef/Owner, The Pipe and Glass Inn, South Dalton, East Yorkshire

THE MAGPIE CAFE

Built in 1750, in the historic port of Whitby, 14 Pier Road began as the home of a local merchant and has had many uses over the years. In the late 18th century, the distinctive black-and-white building was the home of a member of the Scoresby whaling family and later it became The Pilotage. Here, the pilots would wait for orders to bring vessels into the harbour. Later still, it was acquired by Harrowings for use as a shipping office, and it's from that era that the Magpie Ghost (Albert) reputedly originated.

In 1939, The Magpie moved into No. 14 (although there has been a Magpie café in various buildings on Pier Road since c. 1900). The Magpie was purchased in the 1950s by the grandparents of one of the present owners.

We're a family-friendly licensed restaurant overlooking the harbour, with views of the Abbey and St Mary's Church. Given the proximity of the fish market across the road, it's not surprising that we specialise in fresh Whitby fish (up to 19 varieties) and shellfish. Meat eaters and vegetarians are also well catered for!

The Magpie has received many awards and accolades over the years – we recently celebrated 35 years of continuous entries in The Good Food Guide.

www.magpiecafe.co.uk

CULLEN SKINK WHITBY STYLE

This is a rich, delicious soup which will serve 4.

You'll need:
500ml fish stock
1 litre milk
2 large kippers
700g potatoes (1cm dice)
4 shallots (finely sliced)
2 cloves of garlic (crushed)
100ml double cream
salt & pepper
100ml crème fraîche
chopped parsley to garnish

How to do it:
1. Place all the ingredients (except the cream, crème fraîche, parsley and seasoning) into a pan and simmer gently until the potatoes are cooked.

2. Remove the kippers and about half the potatoes. Skin and remove as many of the bones from the kippers as you can and gently flake the meat. Set the meat aside with the potatoes.

3. Using a stick blender, blitz the soup until smooth, add the cream and some salt & pepper to taste, then return to the heat.

4. Add the flaked kipper and potatoes back to the soup to warm through.

5. Serve in soup bowls finished with a little crème fraîche and chopped parsley.

CRAFTHOUSE & ANGELICA

Situated on the fifth and sixth floors of the Trinity centre in the heart of Leeds, Crafthouse and Angelica wonderfully weave together quality food with an understated luxury.

The restaurant, Crafthouse, benefits greatly from the vast experience of Executive Head Chef Lee Bennett, whose worldly ventures have culminated in the production of some of Leeds' finest dishes. Most of Lee's fine food is sourced within the beautiful boundaries of Yorkshire, with the restaurant proud to acquire their milk and cream from a dairy in Grassington, their smoked fish from East Yorkshire, their meats from a butcher in North Yorkshire and fresh fish and crustacean from a seafood connoisseur in Bridlington.

A spectacular Josper oven uses a unique technique which sees meat and fish dishes chargrilled over charcoal at an astonishing 480°C to give the food that extra special flavour – a factor which contributed to Crafthouse being awarded four awards at the 2014 Yorkshire Oliver awards.

And as if you thought it couldn't get better, they placed a superb cocktail bar directly above! The sixth floor plays host to Angelica, which offers patrons a heated 'wrap-around' terrace – providing the most comfortable and mesmerising view of the city.

www.crafthouse-restaurant.com

ROAST COD FILLET, CRUSHED CHARLOTTE POTATOES, BABY SPINACH, BROWN SHRIMP & SHALLOT BUTTER

You'll need:
4 x 160g cod fillet portions
350g Charlotte potatoes
200g baby spinach
100g salted butter
juice from 1 lemon
200g peeled brown shrimps
100g chopped banana shallots
1 head garlic
½ bunch rosemary

How to do it:
1. Peel the potatoes and place into a pan of water. Add the garlic and rosemary with a little salt and bring to the boil, then turn down to simmer gently. Cook for around 15 minutes then check with a knife to make sure they are cooked, but with a little bite. At this stage remove from the heat and leave to cool but in the liquid so they absorb the flavour. These can be done a day in advance.

2. Take a medium size pan and add a knob of butter and a drizzle of olive oil. When hot add the spinach along with a little seasoning and cook out until wilted down.

3. Remove the potatoes from the liquid and using a fork, crush them down. Add a knob of butter and seasoning then reheat on the stove.

4. Using a large non-stick fish pan start to pan fry the fish in a little vegetable oil. Once you have a nice golden colour on both sides, place the fish onto a preheated oven tray and cook for a further 3 – 4 minutes at 180°C.

5. Using the fish pan add the shallots and sweat down over a low heat in the residual oil. Once the shallots have sweated down, add the butter. Continue cooking the shallots until the butter browns then add the lemon juice to prevent the butter from burning. At this stage add the brown shrimps and remove from the heat.

6. The dish is now ready to assemble.

FORSTER'S BISTRO & DELI

Forster's Bistro & Deli opened in December 2012 supported by its parent company, Forster Community College Ltd.

The college was established in 1981 as Bradford Cathedral Centre Ltd, a charity "for the relief of poverty through the advancement of education and training". In 2008, the college was renamed to Forster Community College in recognition and respect of the pioneering work of the Rt Hon William E Forster, who inspired and led change and educational reform in 1870.

Through the success of the Young Chefs' Academy, the college's first commercial enterprise was launched, Forster's Bistro & Deli, providing opportunities for real work experience within the hospitality and catering sector.

At Forster's, we offer a welcoming social hub and bar in the heart of Bradford, with food that's modern and creative, bringing the concept of 'soil to plate' together. College students learn about food growing through our horticulture programmes and maintain our food-growing areas. They work alongside our professional chefs, using locally grown produce to deliver a unique seasonal menu of delectable treats.

9 Aldermanbury,
Centenary Square,
Bradford,
BD1 1SD
Tel: 01274 739 788

www.forstersbistro.co.uk

TUNA STEAKS WITH SALSA

This flavoursome dish serves 4 and can be prepared in 20 minutes.

You'll need:
4 x 6 -7oz tuna loin steaks
1 red pepper
1 green pepper
1 yellow pepper
¼ cucumber
1 red onion
1 lime
1 lemon
2 tbsp chopped coriander
½ red chilli
100ml white wine vinegar
50g caster sugar
pinch salt

How to do it:
1. Finely dice the peppers, cucumber, red onion, coriander and chilli into a bowl.

2. Zest and juice the lime then add it to the mix with the sugar, white wine vinegar and salt (leave to marinate for at least an hour).

3. Season the tuna with sea salt & black pepper.

4. Heat olive oil in a large frying pan. Place in the tuna and cook on a high heat for 2 mins each side.

5. Allow to stand for 1 min, then add a knob of butter and the juice of a lemon.

6. Plate up the tuna and spoon over the salsa. Garnish with a wedge of lime.

THARAVADU

'Tharavadu' means 'family which keeps the values of tradition', a notion which has been wonderfully transferred into this authentic Asian restaurant.

Genuine 'Kerala Cuisine' has been transported to the centre of Leeds, where diners are certain to experience the riches and flavours of traditional Kerala cooking.

All of the restaurant's chefs were born and raised in the Kerala region, honing their skills for many years before treating the good folk of Yorkshire to sumptuous, healthy family cooking. As recipes are passed down through generations, this beautifully authentic restaurant has the ability to transport you to a whole new world.

Tharavadu,
7-8 Mill Hill,
Leeds,
LS1 5DQ
Tel: 01132440500

info@tharavadurestaurants.com
www.tharavadurestaurants.com

KERALA FISH CURRY

A recipe handed down through the ages, this fish dish will smother your senses in tastes and smells from a far and distant land.

You'll need:
250g king fish
30g sliced shallots
10g ginger
3 cloves of garlic
8 curry leaves
50ml coconut milk
20ml vegetable oil
½ tsp turmeric
1 tbsp freshly ground chilli
1 pinch mustard powder
salt - to taste

How to do it:
1. Heat the oil then sauté the shallots, ginger, garlic and curry leaves until a light brown colour. Add a pinch of mustard powder.

2. Add freshly ground chilli powder and turmeric. Add pieces of king fish and salt to taste.

3. Add coconut milk and keep the food on a medium heat for ten minutes.

4. The Kerala Fish Curry is ready!

CERUTTI'S

Cerutti's is based in Nelson Street on Hull's old pier, with picturesque views of the River Humber.

Since opening in 1974, the family-run fish restaurant has been frequented by thousands of people who enjoy and appreciate the extensive range of fish delicacies on offer.
Tony Cerutti has fond memories of the venue's early days. "Mother and Father came to the area in 1958," he recalls. "They were running a hotel in Ripon before that and four Holderness farmers, who had heard about their reputation, went to ask them if they would run The George and Dragon at Aldbrough. They ran it for 28 years and it became famous for good food. My sister Tina and I started working there when we were young children, doing little jobs like washing up."

Cerutti's took off really well, so in 1989, Cerutti 2 was opened at Beverley Station, filling a gap in the market for a fish restaurant in Beverley. In 1999, the C Horse Deli opened next to Cerutti 2, providing a wide range of cheeses and ready meals.

Cerutti's has recently celebrated its 40th anniversary and Cerutti 2, its 25th.

10 Nelson Street,
Hull,
HU1 1XE
Tel: 01482 328501

www.ceruttis.co.uk

RESTAURANTS

40th Anniversary Year

Cerutti's

since 1974

YORKSHIRE LEMON SOLE & CRAB WITH GREEN GRAPES IN A CREAMY SAUCE

This recipe celebrates ingredients from East Yorkshire - lemon sole and crab (caught off the East Coast) and Yorkshire dairy cream.

You'll need:
2 filleted whole lemon soles, skinned (8 fillets)
lemon sole bones (no head)
1 medium-sized crab (dressed)
2 glasses of white wine
juice of 1 lemon
picked parsley (1 pack)
3 black peppercorns
2oz of butter
1 pint double cream
30 seedless green grapes
1pt water
1 chopped white onion
salt and pepper

How to do it:
The sauce can be made in advance and will keep for 4-5 hours.

1. Place the butter and lemon sole bones into a pan and heat for 4-5 minutes without colouring.

2. Add the chopped onion, peppercorns, lemon juice, 1 glass of white wine, some picked parsley and the pint of water, then bring to the boil and simmer for 20 minutes.

3. Peel the grapes by hand or by blanching them in hot water and transferring into cold water.

4. Prepare the lemon sole fillets by laying them flat onto a chopping board, seasoning with salt and pepper then spreading the crab evenly over the fillets before rolling up each fillet.

5. Place into an ovenproof dish, covering with a little white wine and cold water.

6. In a clean pan, strain all the liquid out of the fish stock/sauce, return to the heat, adding all the cream, and simmer until the sauce has reduced to half the original quantity.

7. Cover the fish with buttered greaseproof paper or tin foil and poach in the oven on the middle shelf at 180°C (gas mark 6) for 15 minutes.

8. While you're waiting for the fish to cook, add the grapes to the sauce, season to taste...then enjoy the remainder of the white wine!

Warm 4 large plates then divide the sauce between them, ensuring there are equal quantities of grapes on each plate. Place the lemon sole on top of the sauce (two pieces per plate) and sprinkle with chopped parsley. Serve with seasonal vegetables and potatoes, or a seasonal salad.

THE YORKSHIRE MEATBALL COMPANY

The Yorkshire Meatball Co. is an award-winning, speciality meatball bar & restaurant, leading the fight against average, tasteless balls! In fact, we believe we're the first and only meatball café bar and restaurant of its type in the UK.

Inspired by the casual dining scene of the USA, we've created something that is both cosmopolitan and uniquely Yorkshire! We're family-friendly and offer a great range of freshly cooked, wholesome and hearty food.

Simply put, we're all about balls! Meaty balls, fish balls and veggie balls - smothered in warming blankets of sauce, served on a fresh bed of your choice and washed down with a bottle of locally-sourced Yorkshire ale or glass of wine. In fact, at The Yorkshire Meatball Co. you can have your balls served pretty much any-which-way you like, whenever you like. Yes, that's right, you can even have balls for brunch - Balls Benedict anyone? Our main six balls are all gluten-free and are hand-rolled daily in our kitchen using only the freshest and tastiest locally sourced produce.

Since opening our doors in March 2014, we've won the Harrogate Hospitality & Tourism award for Newcomer of the Year 2014 and we've been shortlisted for the restaurant category in the 2014 Free-From Eating Out awards.

The Yorkshire Meatball Co.,
7 Station Bridge,
Harrogate,
HG1 1SS
Tel: 01423 566645
balls@theymco.com

LAMB AND CRANBERRY BALLS, SERVED ON A BED OF POMEGRANATE COUSCOUS WITH A PERSIAN-SPICED TOMATO BLANKET

This is a luxurious, fruity bowl of comfort food, packed with great flavours that burst out with every mouthful. The key to this recipe is the long, slow cooking process. So relax into it, cook it slowly, and eat it just as slowly!

prep time: 30mins
cooking time: 2 hours
serves: a good hearty portion for 4 people

You'll need

For the Balls:
500g minced lamb
1 onion, finely diced
2 large eggs
2 large handfuls of dried cranberries
1 small bunch of coriander, leaves picked and finely chopped
2 tsp cumin
2 tsp turmeric
2 tsp garlic powder
1 tsp ground cinnamon
4 tsp crushed sea salt
black pepper to season

For the Blanket:
700g plum tomatoes
1 large garlic bulb, cloves bashed and peeled
1 tsp turmeric
1 tsp ground cumin
½ tsp ground cinnamon
2 tsp caster sugar
400g chopped tomatoes

For the Bed:
200ml veg stock
200g couscous
100g pomegranate seeds
1 diced red onion
1 handful chopped coriander
1 handful chopped mint
1 handful chopped parsley
50g toasted almond flakes
juice of 1 fresh lemon
salt and pepper to season

How to do it:
1. Generously coat the base of a large pan with oil and pre-heat over a medium heat.

2. Chop each of your plum tomatoes into 3cm chunks and add these to the pan with your garlic, cooking slowly until they soften and release their beautiful juices.

3. Add your spices and sugar, and plenty of sea salt and black pepper to season, then stir well to cook out the spices for 5 minutes.

4. Add your canned tomatoes, stir well and then cover with a lid – reducing the temperature to very low. Simply simmer the sauce for 1.5 hours, allowing all of the fantastic flavours and spices to infuse. Make sure you stir the sauce every 10 minutes or so to stop it from sticking and if it reduces too much, simply add a little hot water. Then move on to the Balls…

5. Simply add all of your ingredients, except for the oil, into a large mixing bowl and mix really well for 5 minutes. You are looking to bring together a really even, smooth mixture.

6. Pre-heat a drizzle of oil in a large frying pan until very hot. Roll your mixture into balls slightly larger than a ping-pong ball, and place straight into the frying pan. Sear off the balls for roughly 5 minutes on each side to create a lovely crust and seal the meat.

7. Once sealed, place straight into the tomato sauce and allow them to cook for a further 30 minutes.

Now to the couscous…

8. Place the vegetable stock in a saucepan and bring to the boil.

9. Place the couscous into a mixing bowl and pour in the stock. The couscous should not be swimming in the stock, but fully moistened with the stock only just covering it.

10. Cover the bowl with cling film straight away and allow it to stand for 5 minutes. When the couscous is cooked, use a fork to separate it and fluff it up. Then simply mix the remaining ingredients in thoroughly.

11. Add the lemon juice and taste for seasoning just before serving.

ᐴ 1875 ᐳ

THE 1875

Shortlisted as finalists for 'Best Restaurant 2013/14 and 2014/2015 in Yorkshire' by Deliciously Yorkshire, THE 1875 is a genuine Indian eatery offering "Indian Food by Indians".

The restaurant was established in 2011 by Manjinder Singh Sarai, who came to England from India as a young child. Manjinder grew up surrounded by the delicious flavours of his mother's home cooking and, following trips to Mumbai, he made it his mission to bring the taste of Indian cuisine to discerning diners in his adopted country.

Manjinder's ethos is simple: "To let the West experience 100% genuine, bona-fide Indian cuisine, cooked by master chefs from India, but without going to India!"

All the food in THE 1875 is cooked on the premises, using spices which are freshly ground on site and ingredients sourced from local suppliers. A team of master chefs brought over from India, create authentic and mouth-watering dishes free from artificial colourings, additives or preservatives and can accommodate any dietary requirement. Manjinder is currently developing a second, much bigger, city-centre site.

First Floor,
Menston Railway Station,
Station Road,
Menston,
LS29 6JH
Tel: 01943 871811
www.THE1875.com

GOAN PORK VINHO DE ALHO

This dish is representative of the Portuguese settlers in Goa and certainly has a European influence. It is Goa's most popular dish.

You'll need:
2 tbsp cayenne pepper or Indian red chilli powder
1 tsp cumin powder
½ tsp turmeric powder
1 tsp mustard seeds or powder
3-4 tsp raisins
1 lime-sized ball of tamarind, seeded (1 tbsp tamarind paste)
3 whole cloves
½ tsp cinnamon
½ tsp garam masala
¼ cup oil
¾ cup wine vinegar (approx.)
3 large onions, finely chopped
1 heaped tsp ginger paste
1 heaped tsp garlic paste
2 serrano peppers, slit lengthwise (green chillies)
2 large tomatoes, finely chopped
2½ lbs pork, cut into cubes
1 cup boiling water
1½ tsp salt (or enough to taste)

How to do it:
1. Grind together the ingredients, starting from the cayenne pepper and ending with the garam masala, into a paste with a ¼ cup of the vinegar.

2. Heat oil in a pressure cooker or heavy-bottomed sauté pan on a medium heat, then sauté the onions till brown, grind onions to a fine paste and return to the pan, adding ginger, garlic and serranos until golden brown.

GOAN PORK VINHO DE ALHO

3. Add the masala paste and continue frying till the masala is cooked and the oil begins to separate, then add the chopped tomatoes and continue frying till the tomatoes blend in and the oil separates again.

4. Add the pork cubes and sear for about 5 minutes, then add the rest of the vinegar, boiling water and salt.

5. Cook on pressure till done (around 15 minutes), then turn off the flame and let the pressure subside.

6. Open the lid and let it simmer on medium until the gravy thickens, adding more vinegar or salt if necessary (alternatively, if using a sauté pan, bring ingredients to boil, reduce flame to low and cook for 40-50 minutes till pork is tender).

Serve with rice or naans and thoroughly enjoy Goa and India's most popular pork dish.

GIMBALS RESTAURANT

Opened in 1995 by Janet and Simon Baker, Gimbals Restaurant aimed to bring simple yet sumptuous food to the little village of Sowerby Bridge. And boy did it succeed.

With a passion for good food, Gimbals' menu takes its inspiration from what the British countryside and seas have to offer. Changing with the seasons, this restaurant's menu uses Yorkshire elements to create local, handmade and wild dishes.

Janet's innate flair means that honest dishes, whether they be classical or 'unusual', complement the decadent décor, creating a wonderful atmosphere which is perfect for a unique and memorable dining experience.

The inspiration for this dish stems from discovering a jar of Fortnum and Mason's beef tea in the store cupboard. We realised it was a replica of our own beef tea, that we use in the recipe below. Upon it was written that during the Crimean War Queen Victoria ordered Fortnum's beef tea to be sent to Florence Nightingale to nourish her patients "without delay". This heart warming beef tea was greatly appreciated by the injured soldiers and forms the basis of this Yorkshire classic, a no-rush dish but every bit worth the wait.

76 Wharf Street,
Sowerby Bridge,
HX6 2AF
Tel: 01422 839329
www.gimbals.co.uk

SLOW BRAISED BRISKET OF BEEF IN BEEF TEA WITH HORSERADISH ROOT PUREE

Beef in Beef Tea
You'll need:

1kg beef brisket, boned and rolled from your local Yorkshire butcher
1 onion
4 carrots
4 sticks of celery
4 bay leaves

10 peppercorns
a bunch of parsley
a sprig of rosemary
a sprig of thyme
a tablespoon of salt
3 pints of beef stock
1 can of Black Sheep Ale

How to do it:
1. Preheat the oven to gas mark 3 or 170°C.
2. Take a deep casserole dish with a tight fitting lid. Roughly chop all of the vegetables and place in the bottom of the casserole dish.
3. Take the whole joint of brisket and dry fry in a non-stick frying pan until golden brown all over.
4. Place the browned off brisket on top of the vegetables in the casserole dish and sprinkle with the bay leaves, herbs and peppercorns.
5. Pour on all of the beef stock - your beef should be totally covered by the stock.
6. Place the lid on, put in oven for approximately 4 hours, checking it to make sure the juice hasn't evaporated. Top up with water if necessary.
7. Take joint out after 4 hours and squeeze gently, the meat should pull apart easily.
8. Remove the meat from the stock and set to one side.
9. Reduce the remaining stock by half, then add the can of Black Sheep Ale.
10. Reduce the liquor by half again until a nice beefy tasting tea is left.
11. Strain the stock to remove the vegetables and herbs so it is clear. Season to taste.

12. Once the beef has cooled, remove the string and cut into portions. Place the portions back in the dish and cover with the beef tea, pop the lid back on.
13. Turn the oven up to Gas Mark 5 or 190°C, and place the dish back in for a further 25 minutes. (serves 6)

Horseradish Root Puree

You'll need:
150ml double cream, lightly whipped
15g freshly grated horseradish soaked in hot water
1 tbsp white wine vinegar
2 tbsp hot water
a pinch English mustard
a pinch caster sugar
salt and pepper to taste

How to do it:
Drain the soaked horseradish and mix with all the other ingredients

GIMBALS ROCKING RHUBARB COCKTAIL

Here at Gimbals we love to create homemade tinctures and moonshine from the seasonal fruits of our fields. Rhubarb tincture is simple to make and oh so delicious! Simply pick 4 large sticks of pink forced rhubarb, discard the leaves (poisonous!) and roughly chop. Place the chopped rhubarb into a 1L air tight vessel. Cover and fill the vessel with a high proof vodka (it should be one part rhubarb to two parts vodka). Leave to infuse for roughly 3 weeks until all the pink has left the rhubarb, then strain into another jar.

You'll need:

25ml rhubarb tincture
50ml Jamaican ginger beer
50ml cloudy apple juice

Mix and serve over ice!

THE CLEVELAND TONTINE

In 1804, the Yarm to Thirsk turnpike was opened and, before long, there was demand for a resting place on the route. Shortly afterwards, The Cleveland Tontine was built to provide respite and refreshment to weary travellers. The vast open fireplaces, stunning painted ceiling and elegant grandeur of the building all remain, but there is no doubt that much has changed over the years.

Today the Tontine boasts 5 AA Gold Stars and is an award-winning restaurant and boutique hotel. Food is at the heart of the business and the Head Chef and his team deliver an inventive, seasonal menu of locally sourced produce for lunch, dinner and afternoon tea.

All manner of celebrations take place at the Tontine, just as they always have. If walls could talk, they would have many a tale to tell!

Staddlebridge,
Northallerton,
North Yorkshire
DL6 3JB
Tel: 01609 882 671

www.theclevelandtontine.co.uk

HERB-CRUSTED LOCAL HARE, HARE PIE, SAUSAGE AND MASH

For the Herb-Crusted Loin of Hare, you'll need:
20g chopped flat-leaf parsley
100g breadcrumbs
3g lavender ends (optional)
4 loins of hare, cut in half
8 slices of pancetta

How to do it:
1. Place the parsley and breadcrumbs (and lavender ends) in a blender until fine.

2. Preheat the oven to 180°C.

3. Lay out a large piece of cling film, lay the pancetta slices overlapping on top, then place the 2 pieces of each loin on the pancetta with the narrow ends facing to the middle.

4. Roll the loins into a cylinder and secure the ends, then slice the wrapped loin into 4 pieces and, leaving the cling film on, pan fry in a hot pan with a knob of butter and 1 tablespoon of oil until sealed and golden brown.

5. Place in the oven for 4 mins, remove from oven and allow to rest for 8 mins, then sprinkle the crumb mix on the flat side of the loin.

For the Hare Sausage, you'll need:
1 hare leg
100g bacon
50g diced Granny Smith apples
1 clove garlic, peeled and crushed
pinch each of ground mace, mixed spice, fine ground white pepper and chopped thyme
50g sausage skins

How to do it:
1. Place the raw hare leg and the bacon in a food processor and blend, before adding all the other ingredients and mixing well.

2. Place the mix in a piping bag, cut off the end, then push the end of the sausage skin over the end of the bag and pipe the mix into the skin.

3. Twist the sausage every 4cm to make small sausages, chill for 1 hour, then cut into individual sausages and grill until golden brown.

For the Braised Hare Leg, you'll need:
2 hare legs
30g unsalted butter
50g diced carrots
50g onion cut into wedges
2 cloves peeled garlic
pinch lemon thyme
200ml red wine
200ml beef gravy
500ml water
4 x 3cm shortcrust pastry tart case
mashed potato

How to do it:
1. Separately, fry the hare legs then all the vegetables in butter until golden brown.

2. Put the hare legs and vegetables together in the same pan, add the wine and cook until liquid is reduced by half, then add the gravy and the water.

3. Simmer for 2 hours or until the leg meat comes off the bone with ease.

4. Strain the liquid from the pan and reduce to a sauce consistency, then pick the meat off the legs and add to the sauce.

5. Place in the pastry case and top with mashed potato.

Place the loin, sausage and pie
together on a plate and drizzle
with any remaining sauce. Serve
with honey-roasted turnips.
(Serves 4)

LE COCHON AVEUGLE

Le Cochon Aveugle is a small, intimate French restaurant on Walmgate in York, serving a fortnightly changing 6 course tasting menu. This ever developing menu ensures that your palate succumbs to an unrelenting parade of the finest of foods.

The dishes are all based on classic French bistro dishes in concept, but prepared using modern or forgotten techniques. Our aim is to submerge patrons into the experience from the moment they sit down, ensuring a unique and memorable visit each time they dine.

Tel: 01904 640222
www.lecochonaveugleyork.com

BRINED CHICKEN

This dish is inspired by Provençal cookery, as it is light, fresh and intensely flavoured. Brining the chicken will result in the flesh staying moist and tender. Please use organic free-range chicken for higher quality and tastier meat. We think that using cheap battery birds is cooking blasphemy.

You'll need

For the Brine:
295g water
75ml white wine vinegar
125g caster sugar
100g fine sea salt
1 teaspoon mustard seeds
2 garlic cloves
1 bunch of thyme

For the Chicken:
4 free-range chicken supremes
14g unsalted butter
1 garlic clove crushed

For the roasted Courgette:
1kg mixed courgette, (yellow, green, round)
olive oil
sea salt
paprika
1 thyme sprig

For the Olive Purée:
100g pitted black olives
50g olive oil
juice of half a lemon

For the Brown Butter Dressing:
30g unsalted butter
lemon juice
fine sea salt

For the Garnish:
1 handful of mixed fresh leaves
of tarragon, dill and chervil

How to do it
Brine:
1. Combine the ingredients in a medium pan and bring to the boil, making sure the salt and sugar have dissolved. Let it cool and refrigerate until cold.

Brining the Chicken:
1. Put the chicken in a large bowl, add the brine and make sure the meat is fully covered. Place in the fridge for 4 hours.

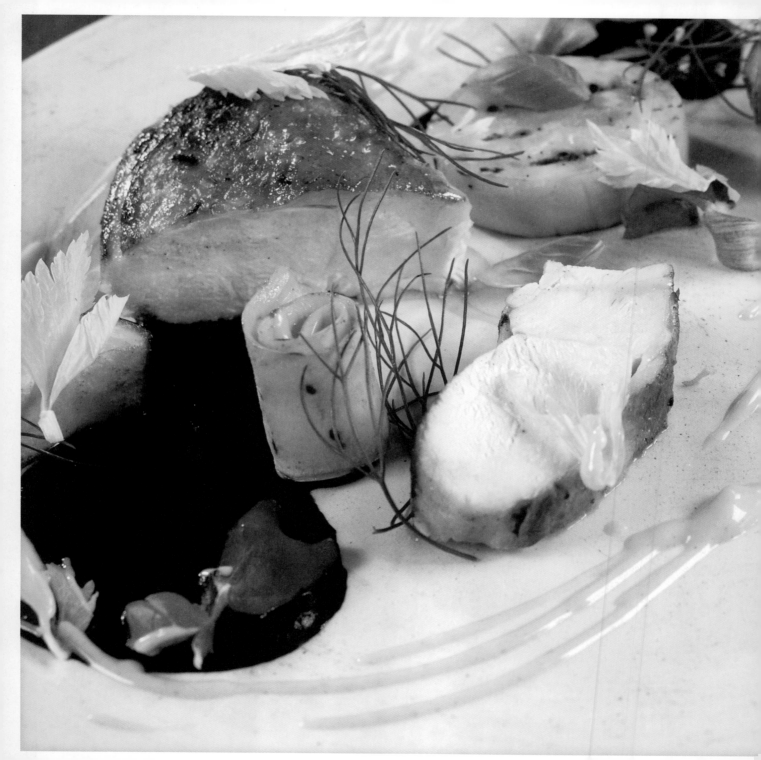

2. Drain the chicken, rinse under cold water, pat dry and place in the refrigerator.

Roasted Courgette:
1. Turn the oven onto 180°C/gas mark 6.

2. Cut the courgette into half-inch thick slices, then place on a baking sheet lined with parchment paper and drizzled with olive oil.

3. Season with sea salt, paprika and thyme then roast the courgette for 15-20mins until just tender.

Olive Purée:
1. Add all the ingredients into a blender and blend until smooth.

Brown Butter Dressing:
1. Heat the butter in a small saucepan over a medium heat until it turns light brown and smells nutty. Whisk in lemon juice and a pinch of salt and set aside.

Chicken:
1. Take the chicken out the refrigerator and pat dry. Do not season the chicken, the brine has taken care of this.

2. Put a frying pan on high heat and add olive oil until hot. Add the chicken skin-side down, and reduce heat to medium and cook for 12 minutes.

3. Turn over and add butter, garlic and thyme.

4. Baste with the melted butter. Cook the chicken for another 5 minutes and then remove the pan and let the chicken rest for another 5-10 minutes.

To serve:
Spread a spoonful of the olive purée on to the plate. Cut each chicken in half and add to the plate. Arrange the courgette nicely on the plate. Toss the herbs in the brown butter dressing and scatter on the plate. Enjoy.

DON'T TELL TITUS
BAR & RESTAURANT

If underlying rebellion is your thing then look no further than Don't Tell Titus Bar & Restaurant. Inspired by Titus Salt, who, despite his many great accomplishments, failed to acknowledge the need for a good pub in the village of Saltaire, this bar and restaurant combination offers the chance to revel in the beauty of the village.

Providing patrons with international tapas, fusion spiced dishes and, of course, fine Yorkshire ale, Don't Tell Titus is a perfect haven for those seeking out good company to go with good food. So next time you're in the area be sure to pop in… but don't tell Titus!

6-7 Victoria Road,
Saltaire,
BD18 3LA
Tel: 01274 595633

www.donttelltitus.co.uk

RUSTIC BEANS CASSOULET

This hearty and enriching meal is ideal to make for guests at any dinner party or soirée you may wish to host. A fine dish, honed and brought to you from the heart of Yorkshire.

Preparation time: approx 20 minutes
Serves 4 as a main course or 8 as a starter

You'll need:
2 sticks of celery
1 carrot
1 small white onion
2 cloves garlic
1 sprig of thyme
1 bay leaf
1 tsp olive oil
salt & pepper to taste
½ tsp smoked paprika
1 tin butterbeans
1 tin kidney beans
1 tin borlotto beans
1 tin chopped tomatoes
1 cup of water

How to do it:
1. Heat oil in a pan. Add diced onion, carrot, celery, crushed garlic, bay leaf and thyme.

2. Heat to sweat off until the vegetables start to soften. Add the paprika and stir through.

3. Drain all the beans and add to the vegetables mix.

4. Add tinned tomatoes and cup of water.

5. Bring to the boil, stirring.

6. Simmer for 15 minutes, season to taste.

Alternatively, to make a meaty main course, add 200g chorizo, garlic sausage, chicken breast or braised pork shoulder when you sweat off the vegetables.

EL-PIANO

We began in 1997 when to use the word 'vegan' was akin to declaring an affiliation with Star Trek! A restaurant serving an entirely plant-based menu was rare indeed, and as we're also entirely gluten-free and palm oil free, EL PIANO is unique in the UK, never mind just Yorkshire.

The result is a multi-award winning eatery where almost anyone with eating restrictions can enjoy everything. For those who have no eating restrictions, our online reviews are testimony to the fabulous flavours we create in our dishes, and we frequently receive praise from even the most dedicated of carnivores.

Not only will we cook up something delicious for you, we can teach you how to do it! We provide cooking classes, cookbooks and special KITS to help you make your favourite EL PIANO dishes at home!

15-17 Grape Lane,
York,
YO1 7HU
Tel: 01904 610676

www.el-piano.com

MEXI TRIO

Refried Beans and Cuban Black Beans on a bed of Rice topped with
Peruvian Green Salsa and Corn 'Worms'
Cooking time 45 minutes
Serves 4

For the Cuban Black Beans:
You'll need
1 tbsp oil
1 finely chopped onion
1 finely chopped green pepper
2 cloves fresh garlic
1 tbsp dried oregano
1 tsp of salt
500g dried black beans - pre soaked
1 glass white wine
water to cover the beans plus 5 cm

How to do it:
1. Add the oil to the bottom of a pressure cooker, add the onion,
green pepper and garlic then sauté for approximately 10 minutes,
until the onion is browned.

2. Next, add the dried black beans. If they are pre-soaked the night
before they will cook faster.

3. Now add the liquid, 1 glass of white wine and water to cover the
beans plus 5cm.

4. Finally, add the dried oregano and salt, bring to the boil and
cook under pressure for 40 minutes or until the beans are soft.

For the Rice:
Measure out dried white rice for 4 people and cook as per the
packaging guidelines.

For the Refried Beans
You'll need:
400g can of borlotti or pinto beans
2 tbsp tomato puree
1 coarsely chopped onion
2 tsp ground cumin
salt to season

How to do it:
Place the beans and all the fluid in a bowl then add the tomato
purée, onion, cumin and salt to taste before whizzing together with a
blender.

For the Peruvian Green Salsa
You'll need:
250g tofu
6-10 cloves of garlic finely chopped
a large handful of fresh coriander chopped

How to do it:
Combine the tofu, fresh garlic and fresh coriander in a blender until
smooth.

For the Corn 'Worms'
You'll need:
100g polenta
100g chickpea or gram flour
a pinch of salt
water to make a stiff paste
sufficient sunflower or rape seed oil to shallow fry the worms

How to do it:
1. Combine the polenta, flour, salt and water to make a stiff paste.

2. Push the mix through a potato ricer into hot oil. When golden,
remove and drain the oil.

3. Arrange the beans on a bed of rice, heat and top with cold
Peruvian green salsa and the 'worms'. Serve and enjoy!

PIPE & GLASS INN

Since taking it over in 2006, James and Kate Mackenzie have transformed the Pipe and Glass Inn from a run-down country pub into a Michelin-starred destination restaurant.

Warm and welcoming in the winter, cool and airy in the summer, the Pipe offers an extensive menu of critically acclaimed food, a well-stocked cosy bar, glamorous private dining facilities, and two (soon to be five) luxurious bedrooms.

Is there any wonder that it's just retained its Michelin star for the sixth year running, and holds the coveted title of The Good Pub Guide National Dining Pub of the Year for 2015?

West End,
South Dalton,
Beverley,
East Yorkshire,
HU17 7PN
Tel: 01430 810246
www.pipeandglass.co.uk

FORCED YORKSHIRE RHUBARB TRIFLE WITH RUM-SOAKED PARKIN CRUMBS AND EAST YORKSHIRE SUGAR CAKES

A truly Yorkshire treat to make for your friends and family.
Makes 4 glasses

You'll need:
10 sticks of forced Yorkshire rhubarb
caster sugar
grenadine
3 leaves gelatine

For the Pastry Cream:
250ml milk
4 egg yolks
65g caster sugar
½ vanilla pod (split)
1 knob of ginger

For the Chantilly Cream:
500ml double cream
½ vanilla pod (split)
toasted pistachios
icing sugar
4 pieces of parkin (see below) or ginger cake
rum

For the Parkin:
200g self-raising flour
4 tsp ground ginger
2 tsp ground nutmeg
2 tsp ground mixed spice
150g oats
200g syrup
50g black treacle
200g butter
200g soft dark brown sugar
2 eggs (beaten)

For the East Yorkshire Sugar Cakes:
250g melted butter
125g caster sugar
375g plain flour
2 nutmegs, grated
10 cloves - crushed to a powder

How to do it:

1. To make the parkin, heat the syrup, butter, treacle and sugar in a large saucepan.

2. Add the flour, oats, eggs and mix.

3. Pour into a greaseproof-lined baking tray and cook for 10 to 12 minutes at 160°C. Remove from oven and cool in tray.

4. Cut the forced rhubarb into 2-inch pieces and place in a deep baking tray with approximately 100ml of water.

5. Sprinkle with caster sugar, depending on how sweet you want it, then pour 4 to 6 dashes of grenadine over and cover with tinfoil.

6. Bake in the oven at 180°C for about 10 to 15 minutes until just poached. Remove tray from oven and cool, leaving the rhubarb in the poaching liquor.

7. When cool, pour off the poaching liquid into a saucepan and reduce to a syrup, then cool.

8. For the sugar cakes, mix all the ingredients together into a dough, then roll into a thick sausage shape and rest in the fridge for at least 30 minutes.

9. Take from the fridge and cut into rounds 1cm thick. Bake on a non-stick oven tray for 10 minutes at 170°C. Cool on a wire rack.

10. To make the custard, whisk the egg yolks and sugar, add the flour and whisk. Bring the milk to the boil with the vanilla and ginger, then pour over the egg mix.

11. Whisk and return to the pan, cook over a moderate heat for about five minutes constantly stirring with a wooden spoon. Pour the cooked custard mix into a bowl and cover with cling film to prevent a skin forming.

12. Cool in refrigerator. Whip the double cream with 50g of icing sugar and the vanilla seeds to soft peaks. Fold a third of the whipped Chantilly cream through the custard.

13. To make the trifles, crumble some parkin into the bottom of a glass and pour on some rum – as much as desired!

14. Stir the gelatine into the rhubarb liquor, then spoon in some of the poached rhubarb. Spoon in the custard, then spoon or pipe some of the cream on top.

15. Finish with the rhubarb syrup and toasted pistachios.

Serve with the sugar cakes.

N.B If you don't want to make the parkin you could use some shop-bought ginger cake.

TOWNGATE BRASSERIE

Since new owner Thomas Hartley re-opened the doors to the Towngate Brasserie, things could not have gone better. Riding high in the TripAdvisor standings, this quaint brasserie hidden in the Yorkshire village of Hipperholme is something of a hidden gem. Towngate Brasserie offers a fine dining experience with friendly and unpretentious service headed up by front of house manager Matthew Morris.

Towngate Brasserie ticks all the right boxes, especially when it comes to the food. A modern British seasonal menu puts great emphasis on locally sourced fine ingredients, which are masterfully crafted together by head chef Will Webster.

All the above is majestically rounded up into a pleasantly decorated building, ensuring that all the senses are given a genuine Yorkshire treat.

2 Towngate, Hipperholme,
Halifax,
West Yorkshire,
HX3 8JB
Tel: 01422 207929
www.towngatebrasserie.co.uk

MILLIONAIRE SHORTBREAD

Serves 4 -5 people

You'll need

For the Shortbread:
90g salted butter softened
50g melted butter to set shortbread
115g plain flour
30g caster sugar
1 vanilla pod (or ½ tbs vanilla extract)

For the Ganache:
300g dark chocolate
300g double cream
125g salted butter
90g caster sugar

For the Baileys Toffee Sauce:
1 tbs black treacle
250ml double cream
100g demerara sugar
50ml Baileys or other Irish cream

This is our take on millionaire shortbread, for this you will need
some form of mould, whether it's some cut-down plastic piping like
us, a glass, or a flan tin (for a flan tin, double the recipe).

How to do it:
1. Pre heat your oven to gas mark 5 / 170°C (fan) / 190°C (electric).

2. Slice vanilla pod in half and scrape the inside into a mixing bowl.

3. Add flour, sugar and softened butter then rub together until you have a crumb consistency.

4. Now bind it together till you have a nice dough.

5. Line a baking tin with baking parchment.

6. Add your mix to the tray and press down so it's flat, bake for 20 - 30 minutes till it's golden brown.

7. Cool shortbread in the fridge.

8. Meanwhile for the toffee sauce, add all ingredients except the Baileys to a saucepan and bring to the boil.

9. When boiled, turn down and simmer for ten minutes.

10. Take off the heat and cool slightly before stirring in the Baileys then put to the side.

11. Take your cooled shortbread and add to a blender in small chunks, blitz until it becomes a smooth powder and then slowly stir in your melted butter.

12. Set in moulds in the fridge, it is up to you how thick you want your shortbread.

13. Now for the chocolate ganache. Bring the cream and the sugar to the boil and simmer for 5 minutes.

14. Add the butter bit by bit, stirring it in slowly and bring back up to a simmer and take off the heat.

15. Again, slowly stir in the chocolate bit by bit till fully melted, leave to cool slightly then add on top of your shortbread and chill.

16. If using a glass or flan tin you would now pour the cooled sauce over the chocolate and set in the fridge. We serve separate as in the picture but this is up to you.

TRENCHERS

Established in 1980, Trenchers seafood restaurant in Whitby is well known throughout the North of England for its traditional menu of fish and chips and many other seafood delights served all day throughout the year.

What better way to get a true taste of what the Yorkshire coastline has to offer, than by devouring fish of the finest quality, which is hand prepared on site, before being cooked fresh to order in traditional beef dripping.

We also pride ourselves on serving fresh salmon, crab and of course mouth-watering Whitby scampi. A restaurant favourite is the delicious steak pie and not forgetting the very popular homemade Trenchers fish pie and appetising fresh crisp salads. There are also a variety of children's meals to excite the younger taste buds.

www.trenchersrestaurant.co.uk

TRENCHERS FISH PIE

You'll need
for Mashed Potatoes:
600g potatoes
300ml double cream
salt and pepper

for Fish and Seafood:
800g fresh cod and haddock or
alternative sustainable species
if preferred
400g fresh Scottish salmon
200g extra large prawns
200g Scottish smoked salmon
100g grated cheddar cheese

for Leek Sauce:
2 bay leaves
200g salted butter
200g plain flour
1pt milk
½ tsp parsley
300g leeks
75g onion

How to do it:
1. Peel and dice potato, boil for 20 minutes. Mash well, adding double cream and season to taste. Set aside for piping.

2. Melt butter in a large heavy bottomed pan. Add the finely chopped leeks, onion and parsley, gently frying for 5-6 minutes. Add bay leaves and flour, mixing well then gradually incorporate the milk, whisking gently. Season to taste.

3. Toss the white fish lightly in lemon juice, white wine and seasoning. Distribute fish evenly between four 7.5" ovenproof pie dishes. Top with prawns and salmon. Then spoon over the leek sauce. Sprinkle with grated cheddar cheese.

4. Pipe or fork mashed potato onto pie. Place on a baking tray in the centre of a preheated oven. Bake at gas mark 5 for 30-35 minutes.

5. Serve with a wedge of lemon and garden peas.

THE OLD VICARAGE

The Old Vicarage restaurant at Ridgeway is Sheffield's only Michelin starred restaurant, where you can be sure of outstanding food and a warm welcome. It is in a delightful Victorian country house in a quiet rural location in the Moss Valley, surrounded by rolling lawns, wild flower areas and hidden copses – a perfect setting for intimate dinners and private parties.

Much like a country house of a century past, the menus reflect the seasons in harmony with its surroundings.

Tessa Bramley, the owner and executive chef works with her chef Nathan Smith who shares her passion for food, and between them they ensure that the Old Vicarage maintains what has become an enviable reputation throughout Britain,

An exciting wine list reflecting the "great and the good" from around the world with fine and rare classics spanning over 50 years and a huge range of affordable interesting wines from boutique wineries, shows an equal enthusiasm for the produce of the vine.

Celebrating 27 years of consistent acclaim by the most well respected food guides and critics, The Old Vicarage offers guests a modern, innovative dining experience. For food and wine lovers, a visit to The Old Vicarage is a truly memorable experience!

"The cooking and the ingredients and the grasp of gastronomy are faultless",
5 Stars, A.A.Gill,
The Sunday Times

www.theoldvicarage.co.uk

ROAST FILLET OF WHITBY COD WITH YORKSHIRE LIQUORICE SAUCE CARAMELISED COB NUTS AND PARSNIP CRISPS

Serves 6
I find it best to prepare all the garnish bits and the sauce first before cooking the fish

You'll need:
6 x 200g pieces of thick cod fillet, skinned and boned
2 tbs olive oil
freshly milled sea salt and black pepper
handful fresh chives, finely chopped

For the Stock:
a few bones to make the stock
½ small onion - peeled and roughly chopped
¼ leek - peeled and roughly chopped
1 stick celery - chopped
1 bay leaf
1 piece lemon zest
5 or 6 black peppercorns
piece star anise

For the Sauce:
small knob of butter
½ small onion finely chopped
2 cloves garlic - peeled and crushed
100g soft liquorice - chopped
150 ml fish stock
250ml double cream
½ lime

For the Caramelised Cob Nuts and Parsnip Crisps:
18 cobnuts shelled
4 tbs caster sugar
1tbs water
2 large parsnips

How to do it:
1. Pre-heat an oven to 200°C, gas mark 6

2. Throw everything for the stock into a pan, cover with water, bring to the boil and simmer for ½ hour. Strain and keep the clear liquor for sauce. Discard the rest.

3. Reduce the liquor down by half to concentrate the flavour.

4. Melt the butter in a pan and fry the onion and garlic without colouring.

5. Add the liquorice.

6. Add the stock and then the cream. Keep bubbling on the heat until it has reduced by half.

7. Liquidise and pass through a fine sieve to remove any bits. Season to taste. Add a squeeze of lime to sharpen it.

8. Dissolve the sugar in the water and over a brisk heat & cook to a golden caramel. Add the nut. Pour on to a sheet of parchment paper to cool. When cold enough to handle, break off the caramelised nuts.

9. Peel the parsnips and slice very thinly using a mandolin. Deep fry half the amount in hot oil until crisp and golden.

10. Drain well and dust lightly with salt. Stir fry the other half in a knob of butter until soft. Sprinkle with a few of the chives.

11. Season the fillets of cod on the underside.

12. Heat a heavy cast or non-stick pan until evenly very hot. Add a splash of the olive oil.

13. Put in the cod, top side down and cook, without attempting to move it for 2 or 3 minutes, until golden. The heat of the pan will ensure that it will not stick.

14. Put the pieces into a roasting tin, golden side up and bake in a hot oven for a further 3 or 4 minutes (dependant on the thickness of the fillets) until moist and just cooked. The fish will exude a creamy residue.

15. Serve on the buttered parsnip with the nuts on top, the sauce around and a garnish of parsnip crisps.

HANSA'S

Hansa Dabhi has been at the forefront of bringing Indian vegetarian cuisine to the mainstream restaurant scene in Leeds and Yorkshire since 1986. Her fine cuisine is based upon the ancient teachings of Hinduism, which state that Hindus are forbidden to kill any living creature, especially for food. Her blend of Gujarati Vegetarian home-cooking, with touches of her East African upbringing, has been highly acclaimed and won her many awards over the years, the latest being voted, 'Curry Chef of the Year' by The Leeds Guide for three years running. Being recognised for 'Outstanding Contribution to the Leeds Restaurant Industry' by the Leeds Restaurant Association in 2008 was the crowning glory of Hansa's achievements to date. Recently Hansa's Restaurant was voted as 'The Best Indian Vegetarian Restaurant in the UK' - by the Cobra Good Curry Restaurant Guide '13/'14. It's the third time she's won this award. She must be doing something right!!

Hansa's also has produced 'Hansa's Indian Vegetarian Cookbook', which she self-published, is highly acclaimed by the food-critics of the Times, the Guardian and the Observer and was voted as the Best Vegetarian Cookbook by the Independent in 2011. She followed it by self-publishing her second cookbook- 'Hansa's, more than just a restaurant, it's my life!'- celebrating her 25 years in business, which has received rave reviews from The Guardian and The Observer as well. Hansa's work doesn't stop there she has also run cooking schools and Hansa and her husband Kishor have also partnered with Kaya Tours Leeds taking small groups on Hansa's Heritage Tours, to give them a real experience of her native Gujarat and other parts of India.

Hansa's is indeed more than just a restaurant!

Hansa's Gujarati Vegetarian Restaurant,
72/74 North St,
Leeds,
LS2 7PN
Tel: 0113 2444408
75 www.hansasrestaurant.com

SHRIKHAND

This is a Guajarati speciality
whipped yogurt dessert.

Serves 4-6
Preparation and mixing time: 30mins

You'll need:
30oz plain yoghurt
6oz sugar
1 tsp cardamom seeds (crushed)
1 tsp pistachio nuts (crushed)
11oz mandarins
(or any other fruit of your choice)

How to do it:
1. Tie the yoghurt in a muslin (cheesecloth) cloth and place it in
a colander.

2. Place the colander in a large bowl and leave to drain for 9-10
hours. The yoghurt will now be reduced to a thick curd.

3. Transfer the curd into a bowl, add sugar, stir lightly and leave
to stand for 20 minutes.

4. Beat the mixture until it is light and smooth, add the fruit and
½ tsp cardamom to the mixture and mix gently to avoid damaging the
fruit.

5. Transfer to a serving dish and garnish with some fruit, the rest
of the cardamom and pistachios. Refrigerate before serving.

LE BOX BISTRO

Le Box Bistro is a Gallic restaurant in Boston Spa, a beautiful village set in the rolling Yorkshire countryside. Le Box serves French cuisine, created with fresh ingredients from the local area. Everything is made from scratch in-house and our menus are based around the game and produce which is available seasonally.

On Sundays we serve a proper Yorkshire Sunday roast, complete with crisp Yorkshire puddings and home-made gravy. Le Box also hosts monthly wine tasting evenings, taking guests around the world with selections of wine and authentic dishes from the tasting area.

This French fancy is a great choice for a romantic meal, a celebration, a friendly catch up or a family Sunday lunch.

Tel: 01937 844 644
www.leboxbistro.co.uk

STICKY TOFFEE PUDDING

You'll need:
For the Date Mixture:
350g pitted dates
1 bottle of chocolate stout
1 tbsp bicarbonate of soda
20ml vanilla essence
1 shot of espresso

For the Pudding:
250g butter
350g sugar
6 eggs
160g chocolate
60g cocoa powder
500g self-raising flour
1 tbsp baking powder

Serves 20

How to do it

Soaking the dates:
Put the stout in a pan and bring
to the boil. Put all the other
ingredients for the date mixture
in a heat proof container then
add the hot stout and leave to
soak overnight.

For the pudding:
1. Put the butter and sugar in an electric mixer using the beater
attachment and beat together quickly until it turns white or for
approximately 5 - 6 minutes.

2. While that's beating together, melt the chocolate and add to the
soaked dates mixture and squish together using your hands so that you
can feel for any stones that may be in the dates.

3. Turn the speed down to low on the mixer and gradually add the eggs
so the mix doesn't split.

4. Keep the speed to low and add the soaked date mixture and mix for
about 20 seconds. Sift the flour, cocoa and baking powder and add to
the mixture with the mixer on low again.

5. When the flour mixture is just starting to incorporate, stop the
mixer and start to fold with a spatula being careful not to knock any
air out of the mix.

6. Line a large baking tin with grease proof paper and pour the
mixture into it and level it off.

7. Bake in a fan assisted oven at 150 degrees for approximately 45
minutes or until cooked.

CAFES, DELIS + BAKERIES

Yorkshire plays host to some great little cafes, delis and bakeries, all of which are ideal to sit in for an afternoon and watch the world go by. This section showcases some of the best places to soak up the enchanting atmosphere that Yorkshire offers - from a day at the seaside to the hustle and bustle of Leeds.

Delicatessens are becoming more popular, full of specialist produce to help you create unique and exotic dishes. As if that wasn't enough we have sweet treats from cafes and bakeries across Yorkshire for you to enjoy in the comfort of your own home!

RELISH

Relish is based in the small historic town of Haworth and was born when we decided to work together, doing what we love most – giving people an unforgettable eating experience. We wanted to offer customers a cosy, home-from-home atmosphere where they'd find great locally sourced food.

With over 15 years' experience in the hospitality industry, we know how to deliver outstanding service by anticipating our guests' needs and treating them the way we'd like to be treated. Our café is family friendly, so parents can enjoy a drink knowing their children will be entertained. Having families of our own, this is really important to us.

Leonie & Joelle
(sisters with a huge passion for excellent service and food!)

69 Main Street,
Haworth,
Bradford,
BD22 8DA
Tel: 07792329524

WHOLEGRAIN MUSTARD AND CHEESE SAUSAGE ROLLS

This is a really easy recipe which can be enjoyed by everyone in the family.

You'll need:
14oz/400g sausage meat
12oz/340g puff pastry
2 tbsp of grainy mustard
3oz/85g strong Cheddar cheese grated
1 egg beaten, to glaze

Variations:
For a different take on the classic, why not substitute pesto for mustard and grated Parmesan cheese for Cheddar cheese? You can use whichever fillings you fancy to suit your own personal tastes.

The sausage rolls can be as big or small as you want – they're great as a nibble for dinner parties or as a Christmas treat.

How to do it:
1. Preheat the oven to 200°C (gas mark 6).

2. Roll out the pastry to a large rectangle, about 3mm thick, and cut in half lengthways.

3. Spread the mustard over the pastry and sprinkle with Cheddar cheese.

4. Roll the sausage meat mixture into 2 long sausages, the same length as the pastry, and place down the centre of each piece.

5. Wet one edge of each strip and bring the pastry over the sausage meat, pressing the edges together. Make sure the join is underneath the roll.

6. Brush with beaten egg. Bake in the oven for 20 mins or until golden brown

EAT ME CAFE

Eat Me Café sits quietly on a backstreet in Scarborough behind the world-famous Stephen Joseph theatre.

We offer a diverse multicultural menu, serving hand-packed burgers, Japanese Ramen, Shetland pies, Thai curries...and much much more. 95% of our food is made in-house from scratch. Our wide range of cakes changes daily and we serve our own much-loved blend of coffee.

We love Yorkshire and Scarborough, and were so proud to receive The Good Food Café of the Year 2014.

We embrace our quirkiness, bringing a smile to our customers' faces from the moment they walk in!

1 Hanover Road,
Scarborough,
YO11 1LS

www.eatmecafe.com

SEAGULL PIE

No seagulls were harmed in the making of these pies!
You'll need:
3 tbsp unsalted butter
3 cloves garlic, minced
1 medium white onion, minced
2 medium sweet potatoes, peeled, cooked and cut into ¾" pieces
1 cup chicken stock
half a cup double cream
3 tsp of plain flour, plus more for rolling pastry
1lb raw fresh chicken thighs, cut into ¾" pieces
half tsp freshly grated nutmeg
salt and freshly ground black pepper, to taste
1 (14oz) pack puff pastry
1 egg, beaten

How to do it:
1. Melt butter in a saucepan over medium-high heat, add garlic and onion, cook for 2 mins, then add chicken and cook until golden (5-7 minutes).

2. Whisk in the flour and cook for 2 minutes.

3. Add stock and cream, bring to the boil then cook (stirring occasionally) until the sauce is slightly thickened (3-4 minutes).

4. Stir in the sweet potato, nutmeg, salt and pepper to taste, adding more seasoning if needed.

5. Heat oven to 180°C, then divide the chicken mixture between four 8oz cocottes or ramekins (set on a rimmed baking sheet).

6. On a lightly floured surface, roll pastry into a 14" square, cut out four 4½" circles, then brush the edges of the cocottes with egg.

7. Place 1 circle over each and press to seal, brush the pastry with egg, then bake until golden on top and the filling is bubbly (20-25 minutes). (Serves 4)

PRIMO'S

At Primo's, we specialise in gourmet hot dogs and classic USA sandwiches, served in a relaxed setting. Our authentic USA-style hot dogs are piled high with fresh, original topping and dressing combinations.

We have a great selection of shakes, smoothies, USA beers and soft drinks...and our coffee blend was the highest scoring espresso at the 2009 UK Barista Championships!

Our Leeds branch is in the iconic Corn Exchange, one of the finest buildings in Leeds.

PRIMO'S SLOW-COOKED PULLED PORK SANDWICH WITH JALAPEÑO SLAW

For the Slow-Cooked Pork, you'll need:
one whole pork shoulder (ask your butcher to trim off the fat)
one whole onion, sliced
two tbsp paprika
two tbsp thyme
two tbsp salt and pepper
½ cup apple juice
½ cup water

For the Jalapeño Slaw you'll need:
half white cabbage
half red cabbage
three carrots
one bunch fresh coriander
two fresh Jalapeño peppers
4 tbsp white wine vinegar
four tbsp mayo
salt and pepper

How to do it:
1. Using a pestle and mortar, grind together the paprika, thyme, salt and pepper to form a powder, then rub this into the pork.

2. Spread the sliced onion on the base of a slow cooker, place the pork on the top, then pour on the apple juice and water.

3. Place lid on, cook for 16 hours on low setting, then remove the pork from the liquid, allowing it to cool before shredding with two forks.

4. Cool the liquid and, when the fat has separated, sieve the liquid back over the pork (this gives great flavour and keeps the meat moist and tender).

5. Finely chop the cabbages, grate the carrots and mix together in a bowl, then coarsely chop the coriander and add to the mix.

6. Deseed the jalapeños, chop the skins and add to the mix, then add white wine vinegar, mayo and seasoning, mixing well.

7. Slice a large roll, place a generous spoonful of hot pulled pork on the base, then top with a lavish spoonful of slaw before replacing the top bun.

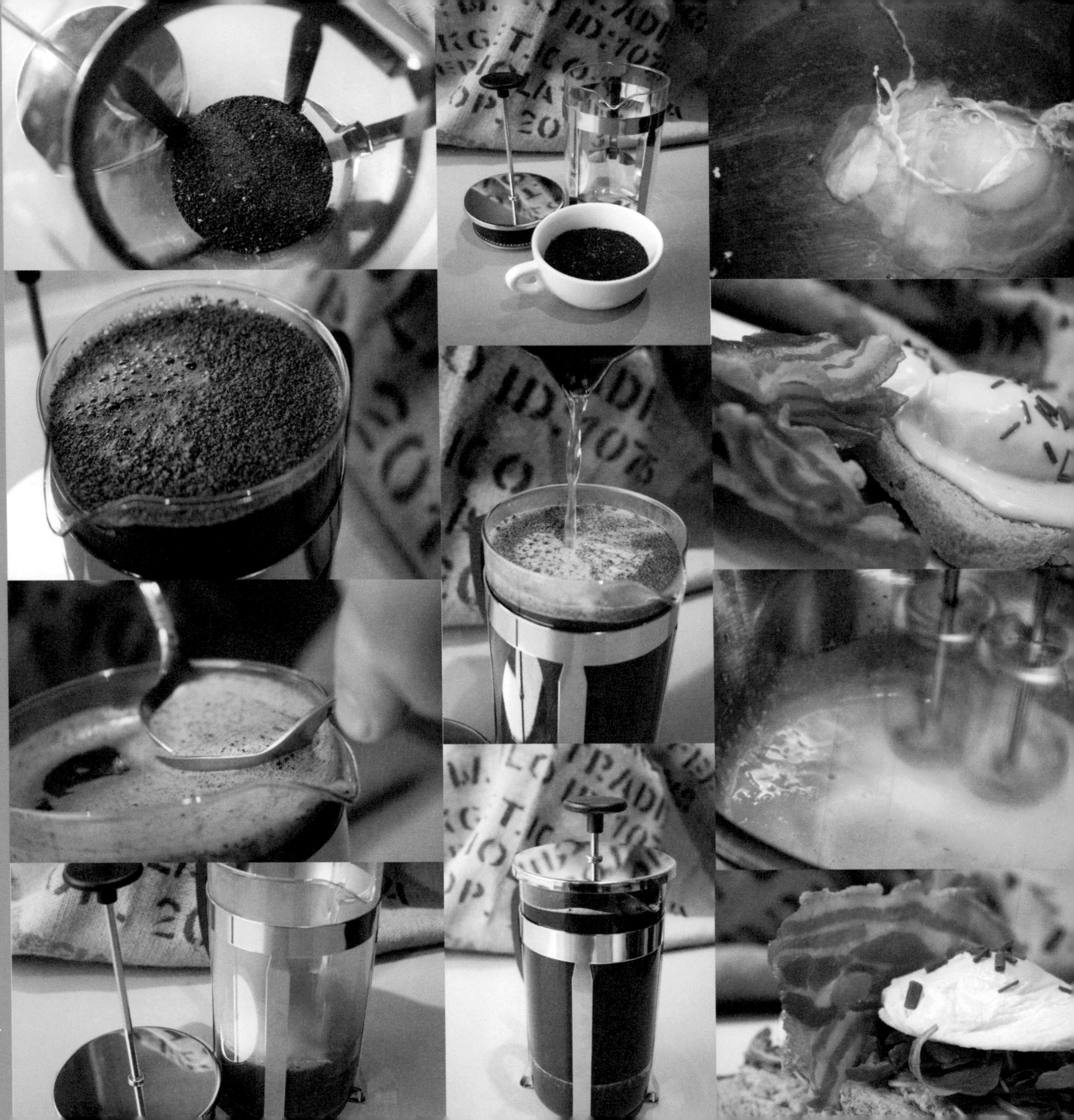

BEAN LOVED

We are Skipton's first independent speciality coffee bar, located just off the award-winning High Street. We're a family-run business, dedicated to creating the best possible coffee experience for our guests, in a relaxed welcoming environment.

Our passion for coffee always has been, and always will be, about freshness and quality. We only buy the highest quality 100% Arabica coffee, that's ethically sourced, direct from the producers...but our passion doesn't stop there. All our baristas have on-going training to build their knowledge and experience. It's our way of ensuring excellence in every cup, every day.

CAFETIERE

We're often asked how to brew quality coffee at home...and actually it isn't as complicated or as expensive as you may think. We suggest whole-bean coffee because all the beautiful flavours and aromas are lost just 15 minutes after grinding.

As a rule of thumb, we recommend 60g of coffee for every litre of water. Pre-heat a cafetière with boiling water, then empty the water and add freshly ground coffee (a very coarse even grind). Sit the cafetière on digital scales and add freshly boiled water to the coffee (this gives a more accurate measure of water and makes for a better flavour).

Wait 4 minutes for the coffee to steep, then gently break the coffee grounds with a spoon (simply run a spoon through the grounds 2 or 3 times). Finally, clean away any coffee grounds sitting on top – this results in a much cleaner cup. Now you're ready to plunge. There shouldn't be much resistance (if there is, try a coarser grind next time). Wait 20 seconds then pour and enjoy!

www.beanloved.co.uk

CAFES, DELIS & BAKERIES

PERFECT POACHED EGGS

We all deserve a little lie in on a weekend, and relaxing with a newspaper while eating a delicious brunch is, in our eyes, the perfect accompaniment. At Bean Loved, poached eggs are the call of many from our brunch menu. Although the ingredients may be simple, the art of cooking the perfect poached egg and hollandaise sauce can be a mystery.

Variations:
Adding smoked salmon, bacon or spinach to your poached eggs, along with hollandaise sauce, transforms the simple egg into a culinary delight.

How to do it:
1. Heat a pan of water until boiling, then simmer, adding a tablespoon of malt vinegar.

2. Just before adding the eggs, turn up the heat (don't boil), stirring the water to create a spiralling effect.

3. Crack the eggs into the water and continue to stir the water without touching the eggs (this will make the egg whites wrap around the yolks, ensuring a soft centre).

4. When the egg whites have turned solid and an opaque white, your eggs are ready.

For the Hollandaise Sauce you'll need:
2 large eggs
2 dessert spoons of lemon juice
113g (4oz) butter
salt & pepper

How to do it:
1. Place butter in a pan over a medium heat and melt but do NOT brown, then transfer to a pouring jug.

2. Place egg yolks into a bowl. (The bowl should be an ideal size to sit on top of a pan of hot water to create a bain-marie.)

3. Add lemon juice and salt & pepper to the eggs and begin to whisk with an electric whisk (a hand whisk can work as well).

4. Continue to whisk until the yolks change to a lighter shade of yellow and start to thicken.

5. Place the bowl on top of a pan of hot, not boiling, water (make sure that the bottom of the bowl does not touch the water) and, whilst still whisking the eggs, start to slowly add the butter (the pour must be a very slow trickle).

6. With a continuous whisk and a steady hand adding the butter, you are looking for a slightly thinner mayonnaise texture.

7. Once all the butter is added, remove from the heat and enjoy.

CRUMBS CUPCAKERY

Crumbs Cupcakery was established in 2010 in a small home-based kitchen. For 2 years, we supplied cakes to people in the West Yorkshire area and beyond. I soon realised I had a passion for creating cakes and cupcakes that made people happy! So...I quit my day job as a marketeer to follow my dream.

After looking around lots of towns and cities in Yorkshire, York seemed like the ideal place to open a unique cupcake bakery. Many a weekend was spent walking around York to find the best location and shop. Eventually, we came across 10 College Street - a beautiful grade II listed building, on the east side of the Minster, with authentic wooden beams, a beautiful fireplace and exposed brickwork. Perfect!

So, after a year or so of preparations (with lots of help from friends and family!), Crumbs Cupcakery opened in July 2012, bringing all those creative ideas to life. We bake fresh cupcakes on-site every day and serve them alongside a vast selection of teas, coffees and cold drinks.

Recently, we converted a 1971 Sprite Caravan called Flo, who sits at the front of the York Minster during summer months, selling drinks, ice cream...and, of course, cupcakes!

Danielle Goodhand

10 College Street,
York,
YO1 7JF
Tel: 01904 638282

www.crumbscupcakery.co.uk

CREME EGG CUPCAKES

These are a firm favourite
at Easter time, but we think
they should be enjoyed
all year round!

For 16 chocolate cupcakes,
you'll need:
80g margarine
280g caster sugar
200g plain flour
1 tbsp baking powder
40g cocoa powder
200ml milk
2 eggs
24 mini creme eggs

For the buttercream, you'll need:
250g softened unsalted butter
500g icing sugar
50g dark chocolate
yellow food colouring (gel colourings work best)

How to do it:
1. Unwrap and freeze 16 mini creme eggs then preheat oven to 160°C.

2. Put the margarine, sugar, flour, baking powder and cocoa into a mixing bowl, then mix on a very slow speed for 10-15 seconds until it looks like breadcrumbs.

3. Measure the milk into a jug, carefully add the eggs, then whisk with a balloon whisk until combined.

4. Put the mixer back on a low speed, add the milk and egg mixture, then mix until combined.

5. Pour into 16 cupcake cases and bake for around 15 minutes* until the cake springs back when touched.

*Halfway through the baking process (around 8 minutes in), remove the cupcakes from the oven, very quickly press a frozen mini creme egg into the centre of each cupcake, then return to the oven to finish baking.

6. For the buttercream, whisk the butter and icing sugar together for approx. 5 minutes to give a creamy consistency, then split into 3 bowls.

7. Melt the chocolate in the microwave on a low setting, in very short (max. 30-second) blasts, add the melted chocolate to one of the bowls, then mix.

8. Add a small amount of yellow food colouring to one of the other bowls and mix.

9. Take a piping bag with a large star-tip nozzle, add a small spoonful of each icing to the piping bag (layering up the different buttercream mixtures), then pipe each cooled cupcake with a swirl of buttercream and top with half a mini creme egg.

Enjoy!

LAKESIDE CAFE

After a stroll around the beautiful Roundhay Park, the Lakeside Café offers the perfect retreat to put your feet up and enjoy a cake (or two!).

The Lakeside is a stylish, vibrant cafe nestled on the edge of Waterloo Lake in Roundhay Park. Looking out over the picturesque lake and woodlands, it offers a wonderful situation to relax and enjoy breakfast, lunch or afternoon tea.

Presenting a mouth-watering array of hot & cold lunches and snacks, wonderful barista style coffee, a fully stocked bar and a delicious display of home baked treats, the Lakeside truly does cater for any visitor's cake-related hankerings, with the Maple & Pecan Triangles (created by our long standing baker Lainey!) proving to be a long-standing favourite. Yum!

Roundhay Park,
Leeds,
LS8 2JL
Tel: 0113 2657338
www.thelakesidecafe.co.uk

MAPLE & PECAN TRIANGLES

This traybake has become a permanent feature in our cookie display counter since its invention.   In fact, it is the one recipe that our customers regularly try to get me to divulge. I have so far kept it to myself....until now. So read on, go shopping for the ingredients, put your apron on and BAKE!

You'll need:

300g dark chocolate
500ml pure Canadian maple syrup
1.5kg salted butter
2 boxes maple and pecan cereal clusters
1kg bag of Swiss style muesli
250g pumpkin seeds
500g pecans
750g raisins
700g granulated sugar
1 tsp sea salt
500g golden syrup
4 tins of condensed milk

How to do it:

1. Grease and line 3 x 9"x13"x1.5" baking trays with baking parchment. Melt 300g dark choc and spread a very thin layer onto the parchment. Allow to cool.

2. Place the maple and pecan cereal, muesli, pumpkin seeds, pecans and raisins in a bowl.

3. Melt 2 packets of salted butter with 2 x 250ml Pure Canadian Maple Syrup. Pour over the dry ingredients and mix thoroughly. Leave to one side whilst you make the caramel.

4. In a large heavy based pan, melt...4 x 250g salted butter 700g granulated sugar, 1 level teaspoon sea salt and 500g golden syrup. Melt all the ingredients. Add 4 tins of condensed milk and bring to the boil, stir continually.

N.B. If you are using a gas hob, I recommend you use a diffuser. This next part is a labour of love....(you may want to pull up a tall stool to sit on).

5. Lower the heat and simmer gently, stirring continuously, for 15 minutes. You need to reach soft ball stage.

6. Carefully pour 75% of the caramel over the soaked dry ingredients and mix thoroughly. Divide the mix into the 3 prepared trays and press down firmly.

7. Put the pan back on a low heat and heat for a further 3 minutes. Add another pinch of salt, stir and pour equally over each of the trays. Spread it evenly using the back of a rubber spatular. (if you use a metal spoon, it will take the heat out of the caramel and will not spread smoothly). Allow to cool slightly for 5 minutes and then mark off your portions and decorate each portion with two pecan halves.

8. When completely cool, glaze with maple syrup to give it a wickedly tempting sheen.

I have not reduced this recipe to a domestic amount as I thought it would make a good display (and lots of money) if you made it for a charity fair. I hope you enjoy making...and noshing this addictive tasty traybake.

FILMORE & UNION

Filmore & Union have invited anyone and everyone to join in their healthy eating revolution! Focusing on gluten free, dairy free and vegetarian foods, these Yorkshire-wide cafés and restaurants aim to help rejuvenate and get you back to your best.

Offering energising breakfasts, life-fuelling lunches and a 100% gluten free a la carte evening menu, Filmore & Union have forged their foods around more Californian-style dishes. Whether you're relaxing and sitting in, or on the go and taking out, Filmore & Union aims to give its diners the highest quality and – most importantly – healthiest meal.

You can find your nearest Filmore & Union branch at:
61 Market Place, Wetherby | 01937 580135
62A Low Petergate, York | 01904 654123
Platform 8, York Station | 01904 634599
3 Station Square, Harrogate | 01423 560988
8 Cross Arcade, Victoria Quarter, Leeds | 01132 441518
6 Harrogate Parade, Moortown | 01132 687805
Unit 2, Newcastle Station | 01912 221684
66 High Street, Skipton | 01756 700738

CAFES, DELIS & BAKERIES

CHICKEN TAGINE WITH DATES AND HONEY

You'll need:

1kg chicken breasts
700g red onion, chopped
50g garlic, finely chopped
1 chilli, seeds in and finely chopped
1½ tsp ground cumin
1½ tsp ground ginger
1½ tsp turmeric
1½ tsp cinnamon
chicken stock
40ml cider vinegar
140g dates, chopped
100g honey
1 tin chickpeas
handful flaked almonds
chopped coriander
handful chopped spring onion

How to do it:

1. Preheat the oven to 180°C.

2. Roast the chicken with all of the spices.

3. Fry the onions, garlic and chilli.

4. Add the honey and vinegar and leave to reduce.

5. Add the stock to cover.

6. Slice the chicken and add to the sauce.

7. Serve the tagine with rice and finish with flaked almonds, coriander and spring onion.

KRAVE

Christian Lambert's wild and desirable menu adds a real whack to Wilsden as Krave aims to generously put a stop to whatever craving you've gathered up at any time.

Whether it be breakfast, lunch or tea, Krave has it all. It boasts a menu which ranges from a no nonsense and hearty breakfast to a wood-fired pizza, and from the most delectable triple-cooked chips to slow cooked pulled pork and chilli meatballs.

Krave is clearly run by a chef who loves cooking, where experimental dishes are intertwined with 'proper food' so that no matter who arrives at Krave, they will walk away overly full and even more so, satisfied.

But fear not, this Yorkshire delight isn't simply limited to Wilsden! Christian takes his supreme 'street food' all around the country to food fairs and country shows, so wherever you manage to spot the culinary genius, be sure to pay him a visit!

www.kravedeli.com

HUEVOS RANCHEROS (RANCHERS EGGS)

This is a fantastic breakfast, lunch or brunch dish that is eaten by Mexican farmers as an all in one pan meal when out working the land on rural Mexican farms.

To bulk up this dish, serve with rice, guacamole or refried or black beans.

Serves 4

You'll need:

olive oil
3 x semi cured chorizo sausages chopped (optional)
2 tins of the best tomatoes you can find (diced small)
1 tbsp tomato purée
1 large red onion diced
4 garlic cloves crushed
half a jar of roasted peppers finely sliced then roughly chopped (wood roasted if available)
3 fresh bay leaves
1 tbsp freshly ground cumin
1/2 tbsp freshly ground coriander
3 fresh green chillies (I like it hot so reduce accordingly if you're afraid!)
4 large free range eggs (the fresher the better, ours are warm when I collect them)
10 stems of fresh coriander
salt and pepper to taste
1 tsp of sugar
100g Wensleydale cheese to serve (or a similar crumbly cheese like Cheshire)
8 x mini tortillas (2 each) or 4 x large

How to do it:

1. Take a large frying pan preferably with a lid, but if not don't worry a plate will do the same job, add the olive oil and onion. If using chorizo add this first on a medium heat to create a nice rich chorizo oil (don't use the olive oil).Sweat the onion off for 5 minutes before adding the garlic then add the dried coriander and cumin before adding the finely chopped fresh chillies.

2. After a couple of minutes, and once you have cooked out the spices, add the peppers, followed by the tomatoes and bring to the boil.

3. Then begin to cook down a little by turning onto a low to medium heat, you don't want to overdo this as it will become too deep and rich and lose its lovely spicy freshness.

4. Once the sauce has cooked down a little, add the teaspoon of sugar followed by the salt and pepper adjusting it according to taste all the time (if at this point you want more heat then add more chilli).

5. Now make 4 small wells in the sauce for the eggs to poach in the wonderful flavoured sauce. Crack the eggs in, working quite quickly, so that the eggs cook evenly and then place on a lid or plate if you don't have one to create steam. At this point you can put the pan in the oven for 5 mins on about gas mark 5 to finish (but I prefer the hob so I can see and control the future of my lovely eggs).

6. Now take a hot pan with a teaspoon of olive oil and start to warm the tortillas one by one then place somewhere warm until you are ready to serve. Once the eggs look just cooked place the tortilla(s) onto your plate and then spoon over the mixture with the eggs and sprinkle the crumbly cheese and chopped fresh coriander.

It's what every morning should be about...the perfect start to the day!

Shibden Mill

PUBS + BARS

The humble public house has been described as the heart of England, and in Yorkshire this is no exception. Yorkshire boasts some of the best pubs in the UK, famous for their northern hospitality, home brewed ales and fantastic grub! Pubs in Yorkshire are the perfect place to refuel after a day exploring the many picturesque towns and villages. Take a seat by the fire, or enjoy breath-taking country views in the beer garden, there really is nothing better than sitting down for a meal in a real Yorkshire pub. We also have a growing bar scene here in Yorkshire, with many serving a diverse range of food to satisfy your taste buds (most likely while enjoying your favourite tipple!).

SHIBDEN MILL INN

The Inn has been rooted in valley life for over 350 years. A string of regional and national awards has extended its reputation nationwide for warm hospitality and premier gastro dining.

Menus change with the seasons to reflect the availability of fresh produce from the surrounding valley and within a ten mile radius; the Inn's own vegetable and herb garden also supplies ingredients for a variety of dishes. Trusted input from local farmers, growers and suppliers ensures only the region's finest makes it onto the plate - food at Shibden Mill is a real 'local affair', the menu awash with seasonal diversity. At the bar is a comprehensive wine list and a fine selection of Cask Marque accredited ales from Yorkshire's premium brewers.

This stylish inviting Inn offers something for every taste and occasion, whether it be a mid-week lunch, evening dinner or a choice from the à la carte menu.

Shibden Mill Inn,
Shibden Mill Fold,
Shibden,
Halifax
HX3 7UL
Tel: 01422 365840

www.shibdenmillinn.com

SALAD OF CALDERDALE CHEESE BON BONS

150g Ivy House Nettle Nipper cheese (Southowram, Halifax)
20ml cream
1 whole egg
100ml milk
100g plain flour
200g panko breadcrumbs
500g large skin-on red beetroots
salt & pepper
100g Denholme Gate apiary honeycomb
50g wild rocket
10g chervil
10g chives
50ml water
50g sugar
zest of half an orange
extra-virgin olive oil

1. Cook beetroots in simmering salted water for one hour, place in
ice-cold water and peel straight away, then place to one side at
room temperature.

2. In a large mixing bowl, place the cheese, cream and salt &
pepper, beat with a wooden spoon until mixed, then place in the
fridge for one hour until firm.

3. Ball the cheese mix into 25g balls, using your hands to make the
shapes, then place in the freezer.

4. Wash the rocket leaves and baby herbs in ice-cold water for one
or two mins to remove any grit or sand, then place in the fridge on
a dry cloth.

5. For the syrup, bring the water, sugar and orange zest to the boil
and set aside to cool to room temperature.

6. To panne (cover in breadcrumbs) the frozen cheese balls (bon bons), place the whole egg and milk in a bowl and whisk together.

7. In two other bowls, place the flour and breadcrumbs, then put each bon bon, one at a time, into the flour until covered, then into the milk and egg mix, then finally into the breadcrumbs, making sure the cheese is totally covered with the crumbs. Fry for 5-10 minutes. Plate up the salad, leaves, beetroot and bon bons and drizzle with the syrup.(Serves 3)

BUNDOBUST

Bundobust started in April 2013 as a collaboration between award winning institutions 'Prashad' (Gordan Ramsay's Great British Restaurant finalist) and 'The Sparrow Bier Café' (The Guardian's Top 10 UK Craft Beer Bars). After a handful of successful and sold out food and beer pairing events, it was decided that a permanent home should be found. In July 2014 Bundobust opened its doors on Leeds' Mill Hill, a once derelict street that is slowly being brought back to life.

Bundobust is not a restaurant, it is a bar that sells Indian street food with an extensive selection of the world's best craft beer. Our food, influenced by the vibrant street food scene of India, should be washed down with hoppy India Pale Ales, a classic beer style that was originally brewed in England and shipped to the troops in times of The Raj. Wine and cocktails are also available.

6 Mill Hill,
Leeds,
LS1 5DQ

www.bundobust.com

ONION GOBI BHAJI-ONION, CAULIFLOWER & SPINACH BAHJI'S

You'll need:
2 onions
1 small cauliflower
1 bunch spinach
1tbsp whole coriander seeds
1tsp ajwain seeds
1 crushed red chilli
2 green chillies (medium)
1tsp salt
1 cup gram flour
handful of chopped coriander
sunflower oil

How to do it:
1. Finely chop vegetables then mix all spices together (coriander seeds, ajwain, crushed red chilli, salt).

2. Once mixed, add all fresh ingredients and squeeze the dry ingredients through the fresh vegetables, encouraging the natural moisture to be released.

3. Cover and set aside for 15-20 minutes. Now add the gram flour and mix through once more, ensuring all the spices and gram flour are combined to form a batter.

4. Now form the mixture into 12 small balls and set aside.

5. Heat some oil (enough to deep fry the bhajis) to 160°C. The bhajis will be quite loose in consistency but don't worry. Reform the shape and gently lower into the oil. If you would prefer this can be done with a spoon but this may not give you the perfect shape.

6. Fry till golden brown and drain on some kitchen paper.

7. Serve piping hot with some yoghurt raita and salad.

THE DEVONSHIRE ARMS

The Devonshire Arms is a family-owned village pub serving locally sourced fine food and ales with quality wines.
We believe that a pub is far more than a place to enjoy a drink and a bite to eat. A village pub is central to the local economy, injecting energy into village life and helping to secure the future of our rural economy.

This is why we endeavour to keep supply chains as short as possible. Not only does it ensure that we get the most fresh and seasonal produce, but that our local economy and people benefit. By working together pubs, producers and suppliers can build stronger local economies, whilst our customers can be secure in the knowledge that we have sourced the best ingredients for their dish. A village pub has always been the focal point of the community. In the Twenty-First Century this means adding value to our local economy.

The Devonshire Arms,
Lightwood Lane,
Middle Handley,
Sheffield,
S21 5RN
Tel:01246 434 800

enquiries@devonshirearmsmiddlehandley.com

BEETROOT CURED SALMON

You'll need:
½ side of salmon
500g of raw beetroot
3g of fennel seeds
½ bunch of tarragon
250g of caster sugar
500g of sea salt

How to do it:
1. Peel the beetroot and cut it into 3cm cubes.

2. Blend the beetroot, fennel seeds, tarragon, sugar and sea salt in a food processor to make the cure for the salmon.

3. Pin bone and trim the salmon, lay it onto a large tray and pour the cure over, ensuring the fish is completely covered.

4. Cover the dish with cling film then leave in the fridge for at least ten 10 hours, giving the cure the chance to completely permeate the fish.

5. After ten hours you may think it's ready to go but at this point you must remember to turn the salmon over and cure for another 20 hours, again ensuring that the fish is completely cured.

6. Remove the cling film, tip away any remaining juices, wash off the cure and pat the salmon dry.

To Serve:
At The Devonshire Arms, the salmon is usually served with a shellfish mayonnaise and crackers. But at home, you can incorporate it into any number of dishes.

Here are a couple of suggestions:

Beetroot Cured Salmon Blinis
You'll need:
1 tub of sour cream
Fresh chives and its flowers

Blinis
How to do it:
1. Cut the salmon across the grain of the fish with a sharp knife.
2. Chop the chives into 0.5cm lengths
3. Combine the chives with sour cream - season to taste.
4. Place approximately 1 teaspoon of the sour cream on each blini.
5. Place the smoked salmon on top of the sour cream
6. Add chive flowers to garnish

Beetroot Cured Salmon and Hazelnut Salad
You'll need:
Beetroot cured salmon - sliced as above
Mixed salad leaves
Watercress (quantities of the above vary to taste)

For the Hazelnut Vinaigrette:
25g Chopped Hazelnuts
10g White Wine Vinegar
30g Olive Oil
10g Hazelnut Oil
Salt & Pepper

1. Whisk the above together. Use to dress the salad.

FARM SHOPS

As the search for locally produced food produce intensifies, so has the popularity of the farm shop – and boy is Yorkshire blessed with an abundance of them!

Our appetite for local food has set off a new trend with farm shops acknowledged for their quality produce that our supermarkets cannot compete with. Through this, farm shops are helping reconnect consumers with their local farmers and producers. This isn't a move backwards, rather forwards with farm shops viewed as much more than meat counters with some expanding fast into ready meals and other growing consumer trends. Most importantly, the hints and tips from expert producers can go a long way to making your dishes extra special!

ASTON SPRINGS FARM

Aston's Restaurant has emerged successful since its opening 18 months ago, with this success being placed largely at the feet of its head chef, Andrew Brooks.

Andrew's passion for cooking developed from a young age, a passion which would see him attend catering college at the age of 16. Upon completing his qualifications, he worked in award winning gastro pubs in and around Leicester, before making the trip of a lifetime to Australia.

It is Down Under where Andrew became a head chef at a spa & golf resort on the west coast of Australia, something which inevitably provided him with the skills and know how to run a fine quality bistro-styled restaurant.

After working in London upon his return, Andrew finally made his way into Yorkshire working at Hendersons as head chef. Before long, he was offered the chance to be head chef at his own restaurant at Aston Springs Farm.

It is this journey which has brought an eclectic and scrumptious feel to the Aston's menu, culminating in a menu which benefits greatly from the onsite rare breed pork and free range eggs. Other local produce are used at the restaurants' weekly bistro and theme nights, ensuring that Aston's is not somewhere to be missed!

Mansfield road,
Aston,
Rotherham,
S26 5PQ

astons@astonspringsfarm.co.uk
www.astonspringsfarm.co.uk

ASTONS ULTIMATE BURGER

You'll need

For the burger:
540g/1lb 3oz minced beef chuck steak
225g/1oz chopped coriander
1 onion, chopped
1 tbsp Dijon mustard
1 free-range egg yolk
1 tbsp olive oil
salt and freshly ground black pepper

For the pulled pork:
oil, for greasing
2kg/4lb 6½oz pork shoulder
1 tbsp chilli flakes
1 tbsp whole grain mustard
salt and freshly ground black pepper
200ml/7¼fl oz white wine vinegar
250ml/9fl oz cider
3 onions, finely sliced
6 cloves garlic, sliced

For the coleslaw:
450g/1lb white cabbage
1 small onion
1 small carrot
30g/1oz sugar
a pinch of cayenne or chilli powder
add a good dollop of mayonnaise
1. Grate the carrot and cabbage. Then finely slice the onion and mix
all ingredients together for a delicious coleslaw.

For the home made chips:
1. 400g/14oz floury potatoes, peeled and cut into thick batons 6cm/2½in
long and dried on kitchen paper

How to do it:
1. Preheat the oven to 170°C/340F/Gas 3.

2. For the pulled pork, oil a baking tray and place the pork shoulder on top. Mix together the chilli, mustard and salt and freshly ground black pepper, then rub the mixture into the pork shoulder.

3. Pour the vinegar and cider over, then scatter over the onion and garlic.

4. Cover with parchment paper, then wrap in foil and place into the oven to roast for three hours. Remove the parchment and foil, then roast for another hour.

5. 'Pull' the pork by sticking a fork in the shoulder and shredding the meat into small pieces with another fork.

6. Place all the burger ingredients in a mixing bowl and stir to combine. Using your hands, shape into four equal-sized patties.

7. Preheat the grill to hot. Cook the burgers under the grill for 15 minutes, or until cooked through, turning once.

8. Heat a deep fat fryer to 170°C/350F (CAUTION: hot oil can be dangerous. Do not leave unattended).

9. Turn up the fat fryer to 190°C/375F, place the potatoes into the fat fryer in batches and cook for 2-3 minutes until just tender but not coloured.

10. Drain onto kitchen paper and serve with a fresh breadroll with the pulled pork piled high. You can add a simple side salad to accompany the chips and coleslaw.

KEELHAM FARM SHOP

Siblings Victoria and James are the third generation of the Robertshaw family to take over the family business. Keelham stocks products from over 400 local producers and farmers. The award-winning business is entering an exciting new chapter of its story. This will see it extend its operation, opening a second outlet with a cookery school and café, in Skipton in early 2015.

Keelham Farm Shop
Brighouse & Denholme Road,
Thornton,
Bradford,
BD13 3SS
Tel: 01274 833472

www.keelhamfarmshop.co.uk

KEELHAM YORKSHIRE TAPAS

Taste comes first at Keelham, so this recipe celebrates not just Yorkshire food, but the best Yorkshire food. These dishes are great for sharing with friends and family and are simple to prepare in advance.

Jason Wardill, Chef at Keelham Farm Shop

All the recipes serve 6 people with healthy appetites!

For the Blue Cheese & Keelham Bacon Fritters, you'll need:
250g Yorkshire blue cheese
175g dry-cured bacon, diced
120g Parmesan cheese, grated
4 eggs, beaten
10 tbsp cornflour
2 tsp salt
1 pinch oregano (dry or fresh)
1 cup vegetable oil for frying

123

How to do it:
1. Mix together all the ingredients (except the oil) to make a creamy dough.

2. Heat the oil in a heavy frying pan, shape the dough into teaspoon-sized quenelles, then fry until golden.

3. Place the cooked fritters onto kitchen roll to remove excess oil, then serve warm with Keelham's homemade tomato chutney.

For the Yorkshire Oak Roast Salmon Fish Cakes, you'll need:
450g Yorkshire oak-roasted flaked salmon
1 handful chives, finely chopped
2 level tsp fresh parsley, chopped
65g butter, softened
275g mashed potatoes
2 level tbsp plain flour
2 eggs, beaten
125g fresh breadcrumbs
1 cup vegetable oil for frying
salt & ground black pepper to season

How to do it:
1. Mix together the salmon, chives, parsley, butter and mashed potatoes in a bowl, season the mixture to taste, then divide into twelve cakes approx. 3cm diameter by 2cm deep.

2. Coat the cakes by dipping into flour, egg and breadcrumbs in turn, then leave to chill in the fridge for at least 2 hours.

3. Shallow fry the fishcakes in hot oil until golden, then serve warm with lemon mayonnaise and a wedge of lemon.

For the Keelham Lamb Kofta, you'll need:
500g Yorkshire lamb mince
1 tsp ground cumin
2 tsp ground coriander
2 garlic cloves, crushed
5g fresh mint, finely chopped

How to do it:
1. Mix all the ingredients together until blended, divide the mixture into 6 balls and shape into sausages.

2. Thread a wooden or metal skewer through the centre of each and brush with oil, then cook on a very hot griddle for 3-4 minutes on each side (delicious with an apricot or redcurrant dipping sauce!).

For the Yorkshire Goat's Cheese Crostini, you'll need:
150g Yorkshire goat's cheese
3 peppers, a mix of colours works best
baguette, sliced and toasted with olive oil
40ml basil pesto
½ tsp fresh thyme

(for the marinade)
black pepper, freshly ground
¼ tsp sea salt
1 tsp fresh thyme
3 tbsp balsamic vinegar
2 tbsp extra-virgin olive oil

How to do it:
1. Grill the peppers for approx. 15-20 minutes until charred all over, put the charred peppers into a heatproof bowl, then cover with cling film and leave until they are cool enough to handle (about 30 mins).

2. Whilst you wait for the peppers to cool, make the marinade by mixing the vinegar, olive oil and thyme in a large bowl, then season with salt and black pepper.

3. Skin and deseed the peppers, cut into thin strips, then add the peppers to the marinade and marinate in the fridge (anything from 1 hour to 3 days!).

4. To assemble the crostini, spread a generous layer of goat's cheese on a slice of toasted baguette, sprinkle with thyme, top with a tangle of marinated peppers and half a teaspoon of pesto, then season with black pepper.

BLACKER HALL FARM

Blacker Hall Farm Shop opened 15 years ago and is dedicated to delivering delicious, award-winning, local food. Winner of the UK's Best Farm Shop (FARMA, 2014), Blacker Hall originally opened to sell high quality meat from the family's own farm, direct to the public.

Now, it hosts a craft butchery counter, artisan bakery, delicatessen and green grocer, as well as the beautifully and sympathetically restored Barn Café, where over 80% of the produce sold is handmade on site by a team of 130 people!

The Barn Café opened 3 years ago and provides a chance for customers to enjoy seasonal, freshly prepared food, largely using delicious ingredients from The Farm Shop.

Blacker Hall Farm Shop,
Branch Road,
Calder Grove,
Wakefield
WF4 3DN

Tel: 01924 267202
www.blackerhall.com

BEEF & CHORIZO CASSEROLE

Prep Time: 20 minutes
Cooking time: 2.5-3 hours
Serves 4

You'll need:
500g beef casserole cubes
½ pack chorizo, sliced
(c. 100g)
1 onion, roughly chopped
1 carrot, sliced
125ml beef stock
1 glass of red wine
1 bouquet garni

How to do it:
1. Pre-heat your oven to 160°C/gas mark 3.

2. Place the cubed casserole beef in an oven proof casserole dish with a little cooking oil and brown the beef all over for a few minutes.

3. Add in the roughly chopped vegetables, bouquet garni, glass of red wine, beef stock and chorizo, and bring to the boil in the pan. Once boiling put the lid on the pan and place in your oven.

4. Cook in the oven for an hour. Stir your casserole at this point and check the liquid levels, making sure your casserole doesn't boil dry. If it does, add a little water to the pan. Check the casserole again after another hour and return back to the oven. Cook for a further half an hour to an hour (total 2.5 to 3 hours). After this time, remove the bouquet garni.

Serve with home-made dumplings, available to pick up from The Delicatessen. This is a seasonal casserole so feel free to add extra seasonal veg.

Wine Suggestion:
Sierra Grande Merlot available from The Wine Loft at Blacker Hall.

FARMER COPLEYS

Farmer Copley's strive to provide the very best quality products that can be used by you in fantastic dishes, capturing flavours which are to be relished.

The Farm Shop stocks products such as pork, beef and even pumpkin, all of which are produced either on site or locally, ensuring that any diner is sure to receive the best that Yorkshire has to offer.

Having been awarded the Best Farm Shop in the UK, Farmer Copley's reputation has gone from strength to strength since it opened in 2003, culminating in creating the Denby Dale Pie in 2012 - a 3 tonne pie including 9 different meats!

2009 saw the introduction of our long awaited Moo Café which was built for a cup of tea and a slice of cake. The café has been a major success and we put this down to the simplicity of the café & farm shop ethos. There is nothing complicated at Farmer Copley's it is simply home and locally sourced foods, prepared fresh.

www.farmercopleys.co.uk

MRS COPLEY'S VENISON & BEETROOT BURGER WITH 'SKIN ON' CHIPS & MANGO RELISH

You'll need:

375g minced venison
1 small shallot
1 bunch fresh beetroot with leaves
6 sprigs of fresh thyme
middle of bread
salt & pepper
1 free range egg yolk
1 tbsp soft brown sugar
2 tsp white wine vinegar
½ a fresh mango cubed
zest of one third of an orange
juice of 2 oranges
3 tbsp water
splash olive oil
some red skinned potatoes
5 bread cakes

How to do it:

1. Wash potatoes and cut into chunky chip lengths. Blanch cut chips in fryer for 6 mins at 130°C, then set to one side. Just prior to serving, pop chips back into fryer for a further 4 mins but this time on a heat of 180°C and stack neatly.

2. Boil the beet for 30 mins and leave to cool for a further 30. Take one of the beets and slice thinly - this will go on top of the bread cake but under the burger. Dice the rest finely and set to one side.

3. Cut top leaves from beet, wash and cut into juilliens and fry on 180°C for about 10 seconds until crispy. Put to one side for the finished dish on a piece of kitchen roll to soak any excess oil and sprinkle with a dash of salt.

4. Get a dry bowl ready to put ingredients in for venison burger. Pop the minced venison into the bowl. Finely dice the shallot and add to bowl. Wash and finely chop the thyme and again add to bowl. Add the egg yolk and a handful of breadcrumbs - just pull from the middle of bread and dice (if you use old bread this will aid digestion!) Next add the diced beetroot and then slice. You could use grated beet but I like the texture of the diced beet that it brings to the dish.

5. Mix all the ingredients in the bowl exceedingly well by hand, and then season to taste with salt & pepper, then set to one side to rest whilst you make the mango relish.

6. Peel and cube half a mango.

7. Take your oranges and take the zest from a third of an orange skin, making sure there is no pith as it tastes bitter.

8. Pop a frying pan on the heat, add a splash of olive oil, add the mango and the zest and sweat off until the juices start to release. Once it starts to sizzle add the juice of both oranges. Next add the white wine vinegar and a pinch of salt, the water and add a dash of brown sugar. Turn down the temperature and let reduce.

9. Back to the venison...take some mixture pat into shape and then fry in pan, sealing the meat. I suggest serving it pink but note it will look pink due to the beet. Pop the chips in on high temperature and then plate up and enjoy.
To plate up, stack in following order... bread, sliced beet, venison burger, mango relish, beet leaves, bread and chips to one side.

N.B. I cannot take 100% of the credit for this recipe, it was a meeting of minds between myself and Mo, the new head chef of Moo Cafe, a formidable team I feel.

STREET
FOOD

Street food is a huge growing trend in the UK and isn't to be confused with the 'greasy burger vans' that you might find on the road side. Street food today is recognised for its high quality and use of great local produce with truly authentic and affordable dishes being served from around the world here on our streets in the UK. From bangers and mash, to Baltis and Bhajis, tea cakes to tacos, the choice of cuisines on offer is huge.

Attracting Michelin starred chefs, Master Chef winners and finalists to enthusiastic 'foodie' types, the calibre of street food offered is a 'country mile' better than traditional fast foods!

134

BELGRAVE MUSIC HALL & CANTEEN

Located in Leeds' vibrant Northern Quarter, the building first opened its doors in 1934 as Leeds Children's Palace, a 3-storey recreation hall and nursery which was built to provide childcare support for the working families of Leeds.

After many years of neglect, the building has been restored to its former glory and reopened as Belgrave Music Hall & Canteen. Spread over three floors, the venue comprises two bars, two kitchens, event spaces and a spectacular roof terrace hosting live music, comedy, film and art exhibitions...as well as serving fresh, canteen-style food, amazing cask ales and premium craft beers.

1A Cross Belgrave St, Leeds, West Yorkshire, LS2 8JP
Tel: 0113 2346160

www.belgravemusichall.com

STREET FOOD

FU-SCHNIKENS

This recipe by Ben Davy, for sticky nam pla & palm-sugar wings, is an adaptation of the Pok Pok classic. It's easy to make and is done in stages over a day...the end result is well worth the wait!

(Serves 4-6)

You'll need

For the wings:
20-30 free-range chicken wings, tips removed
3 litres vegetable oil (or enough to cover the wings)

For the brine:
400ml Nam Pla
3 cloves garlic
2 tbsp palm sugar, grated
1 tbsp salt
200ml warm water

For the glaze:
400ml fish sauce
100ml water
200g palm sugar
2 tbsp chilli paste

For the garnish:
coriander
black & white sesame seeds
sliced spring onion

How to do it:
1. For the brine, roughly chop the garlic, place a little pile of salt on the chopping board, then use the flat of the knife to grind the garlic over the salt until you have a purée (the salt will act as sandpaper).

2. Add the garlic to the warm water and infuse for 10 mins, then strain and remove the garlic, reserving the water.

3. Mix the garlic water, nam pla and sugar together, chill, then add the wings, mix well and refrigerate for 12 hours. (This process will brine the wings, resulting in an incredible texture and flavour.)

4. Confit the wings by removing them from the brine and patting them dry, placing them in a deep pan, then covering them with vegetable oil.

5. Cook on a moderate/gentle heat for 2-3 hours or until the meat starts to come away from the bone. Carefully lift the wings out of the oil and chill.

6. For the glaze, add all the glaze ingredients to a saucepan and reduce on a high heat to a sticky, almost caramel-like, consistency. (Test by drizzling a little bit on a work surface to cool it quickly, then you'll safely be able to dab it with your fingers and see if it's the right stickiness.)

7. Taste as you go, adjusting the sugar levels as necessary. (If it's too salty add more water, and if not sweet enough add more sugar.)

8. When the glaze is done, keep it in a pan until you need it.

9. Fry the wings in small batches using a clean deep fat fryer at 170°C, till they're a deep golden brown colour and nicely crisp, then lift the basket out and drain on kitchen paper.

10. To finish, toss the wings in the glaze and garnish with toasted black and white sesame seeds, finely sliced spring onions and coriander...then serve with loads of cold beer!

Image courtesy
of Giles Rocholl

PHO
(TRINITY KITCHEN)

We founded Pho in 2005, after travelling to Vietnam and falling in love with the country's national dish, pho [pronounced 'fuh'].

Pho is located at the entrance to the amazing Trinity Kitchen food court and specialises in great-value Vietnamese street food. Our menu includes spicy Vietnamese curry and salads, wok-fried noodles, fresh juices and Vietnamese beers...and of course, a variety of different types of pho - an amazingly tasty and nutritious noodle soup.

Stephen and Jules Wall

Trinity Kitchen, Leeds, LS1 5AY
Tel: 0113 834 5029
www.phocafe.co.uk
@PhoRestaurant (Twitter/Instagram/Facebook)

PHO GA
(VIETNAMESE CHICKEN NOODLE SOUP)

You'll need:
chicken bones, whole carcass
we recommend you roast a whole chicken, use the carcass for the stock, then add the meat to each bowl of pho
2 large pieces cinnamon
4 pieces star anise
5 black peppercorns
10 coriander seeds
1-2 cloves
4 inch ginger
1 white onion, cut in half

2 red shallots, cut in half
1 garlic bulb, broken into whole cloves
salt and sugar for seasoning
fish sauce

How to do it:
1. Place the chicken carcass in a large stockpot, fill the pot with water, then bring to the boil.

2. Cut the ginger in half lengthways and bash it with a rolling pin, then roast the ginger, garlic and shallots in a dry hot wok until a little charred.

3. Add cinnamon, star anise, peppercorns and cloves to the wok and dry roast for a minute or two.

4. As the water reaches a simmer, if you are starting with raw bones, skim foam that forms. Then add all the spices.

5. Bring back to the boil (uncovered), then reduce the temperature to its lowest and simmer for 2-3 hours. Add a little more water if needed.

6. Drain through a fine sieve or chinois to get a clear stock, then return the stock to the pot and season with salt, fish sauce and sugar.

7. The stock is ready to serve or cool quickly, cover and refrigerate.

Pour the stock over blanched Banh Pho noodles and sliced cooked chicken, then garnish with thinly sliced white onion and spring onion. Serve piping hot with a side plate of fresh herbs (coriander, mint, Thai basil), beansprouts, sliced red chillies and a wedge of lime (added throughout the meal to tailor the bowlful). Build on the flavour with a second helping of hot stock, more fish sauce, a spoonful of rice vinegar for sourness, Sriracha chilli sauce or even a raw egg yolk.
(Serves 4)

Image courtesy of
Paul Winch-Furness

ROLA WALA

Epic street-food flavours, discovered on Kolkata backstreets, Bombay beaches, and Keralan waterways, led Aussie, Mark Wright, on a journey to bring the incredible experience of Indian street food back to the UK.

Arriving back in London from India in 2012, the burgeoning British street-food industry provided the perfect vehicle to realise his ambition. Mark was able to test ideas and connect with like-minded people while having a lot of fun at the very coalface of Britain's lunchtime market.

Rola Wala (Hindi for The Man that Rolls) was born in 2013 and, later, was named runner-up 'Best Street Food' by the Young British Foodies. Zagat listed Rola Wala in their "Top 5 next-wave names to know".

In April 2014, Rola Wala took on a residency at Trinity Kitchen in Leeds and, following an incredible response, was invited back to set up their first permanent bricks-and-mortar site.

With Danny Vilela taking the reins in the kitchen and Mark leading the charge on the service line, Rola Wala Leeds captures the heart and soul of the street-food experience. What started as a passion project is, today, the result of the collective energy of an entire team that brings high-quality, fresh Indian flavours to punters across the UK. Its mission is to ignite spaces everywhere with incredible Indian flavours. It really is that simple.

www.rolawala.com

MARK & DANNY'S EPIC BREAKFAST NAAN ROLL FLIP

This makes for an EPIC breakfast. It's a bit Indian, a bit British...and a lot of fun to experiment with spices – don't mess up on the flip!

Serves two hungry punters.

You'll need:
(the fresh bits)
4 eggs
½ a red onion
thumbnail of ginger
¼ red pepper
½ diced tomato
small red chilli
coriander stem
clove of garlic

(the spices)
1 tsp cumin powder
1 tsp cumin seeds
½ tsp nigella seed
¼ tsp coriander powder
¼ tsp turmeric

(to cook)
glug of rapeseed oil

(to serve)
black salt & pepper (normal salt will do!)
1 pan-sized naan bread or chapatti (we use fresh – but a roti or chapatti from the supermarket is fine too)
loads of fresh coriander
tomato and chilli sauce
natural yogurt

How to do it:

1. Set a pan on high heat, add cumin seeds and dry roast until they release their aroma (don't burn!), then remove and set aside.

2. Turn the pan down to medium heat, add rapeseed oil, then gently sweat the onion, ginger, red pepper, tomato, chilli and coriander stalk for a couple of minutes.

3. Add cumin powder, coriander and turmeric, cook for a further minute (stirring so spice mix coats it all), then add the garlic and cook for 30 seconds longer.

4. That's your base done, so remove from the heat and leave to cool.

5. Break eggs into a bowl, mix together with a fork, add nigella, roasted cumin, salt, pepper and veg. base, then leave to infuse for a few minutes.

6. Throw it all in the pan with a bit of butter and leave on a medium heat.

7. Place naan over the omelette while the top is still wet, continue cooking until the egg has cooked, then flip it over so the bread is in the bottom of the pan.

8. To serve, remove from pan, top with chutney, coriander, raita and sauces, then roll it all up and eat!

COBBLE KITCHEN

I love food...in every sense! There aren't many moments in the day when I'm not thinking about what I'm going to cook or eat next! I have been baking since I was a little girl, always experimenting with new ingredients and cookbooks. I always struggled to follow the recipes without adding my own twist... and I still do! I'm interested in which new products are available, visiting exciting cafés and restaurants and trying local delicacies, wherever I am in the world!

In early 2013, I went to Ballymaloe Cookery School in Southern Ireland and Betty's of Harrogate. I came home buzzing with inspiration to serve simple, high-quality menus in a relaxed way — the very heart of Cobble Kitchen. I'm passionate about wholesome English fare and comforting dishes that leave you with a big smile on your face!

Cobble Kitchen is based in Skipton, on the edge of the beautiful Yorkshire Dales, and we cater for all kinds of occasions. Our gorgeous homemade goodies showcase locally-produced, seasonal ingredients. They're served, along with freshly roasted coffee, from Marcel, our little vintage café on wheels!

Marcel is a 1955 Citroën H van who, when we found him, was minus an engine and hadn't been driven since 1984. It took nearly a year of hard work to get him back on the road. Marcel is in magnificent shape now and you can see him and sample Susie's coffees and creations at events around Yorkshire. Find out where they are by following them on social media.

www.cobblekitchen.com

SUPER-EASY, OH-SO-TASTY RASPBERRY & ALMOND CAKE

One of my all-time favourites, this gorgeous cake is ideal for all occasions, has a heavenly jammy middle and (shhh...our secret!) is really easy to make.

You'll need:
140g/5oz ground almonds
140g/5oz softened butter
140g/5oz golden caster sugar
140g/5oz self-raising flour
2 eggs
1 tsp vanilla extract
250g raspberries
a handful of flaked almonds to scatter on top

Variations:
Any seasonal soft fruit can be used instead of raspberries. Try cherries, blackberries, plums, pears...or a delicious combination.

You could add white chocolate, use other types of ground nuts or switch the flour for gluten free.

How to do it:
1. Preheat your oven to 180°C and line a tin with parchment paper. A 20cm round, deep cake tin is ideal, but the mix also works well as a tray bake (use a 20cm square tin for about 9 pieces of cake). Alternatively, you could make mini loaves or muffins.

2. Put all the ingredients, except for the raspberries and flaked almonds, into a big bowl and mix them thoroughly by hand or with a mixer. This will give a thick sticky batter.

3. Carefully spread half the mix into the bottom of the tin. It should be just enough to cover most of the area.

4. Sprinkle in the fruit, then dollop the remaining mix on top, spreading it over the fruit. This is a sticky job and much easier with your fingers! It's OK if some of the fruit is exposed or the mix is unevenly spread. The cake will sort itself out as it rises!

5. Scatter on the almonds and pop the cake in the oven for 40-50 minutes until golden.

6. Leave it to cool, then dust with icing sugar and serve with a good brew. It's also perfect as a pudding, straight from the oven with cream or ice cream.

I LOVE CHEESECAKE

In October 2013, I Love Cheesecake made its debut at Upmarket Sunday in Huddersfield to a sell-out crowd! One hectic year on, my business is growing into a successful family enterprise.

I was born and brought up in Huddersfield and I've always been a keen baker, spending many a school lunch time reading cookery books! Something I still like to do now. After taking time out to look after my two children, I wanted to do something I loved – and with cheesecake being one my family's favourite desserts, I Love Cheesecake was born.

At I Love Cheesecake we make individual cheesecakes from traditional to quirky - there really is a flavour to tantalise every taste bud! From Liquorice and Blackcurrant to Lemon and Ginger, our cheesecakes are perfectly chilled and packed with flavour. Using local produce is also high on our priority list with all of our cakes made using Holmfirth's Longley Farm soft cheese and cream, and with fruit grown in our kitchen garden.

You can find us: In Huddersfield train station every Fri 4pm-6.30pm, Cleckheaton Farmers Market 9am-1pm and Huddersfield Upmarket Sunday – 2nd Sunday of every month.
Tel: 07715 107502

www.ilovecheesecake.co.uk
facebook:Ilovecheesecake/huddersfield
twitter:lovincheesecake

CHOCOLATE CHEESECAKE BROWNIE

There's brownie, then there's 'cheesecake brownie', so much better!
Gooey brownie swirled with a baked vanilla cheesecake top.

Tin size: approx. 21 x 30 cm
(the recipe could be halved for a smaller tin)
Time: 10 mins prep + 35/45 mins cooking
Servings: will cut into 15 generous squares, but could be cut into 60 mini pieces.
Note: if you want to cut into mini pieces, cut into 15 first then refrigerate before cutting into smaller pieces.

You'll need for the Brownie:
140g plain flour
230g dark chocolate
Handful of milk chocolate buttons
170g unsalted butter
260g light brown sugar
4 eggs

For the Cheesecake Top:
2 eggs
80g caster sugar
300g cream cheese
2 tbsp plain flour

How to do it:
1. Preheat the oven to gas mark 4/180°C.

2. Grease and line the tin.

3. Place all the cheesecake top ingredients in a mixing bowl, beat to together until smooth and set aside.

4. Place the chocolate and the butter in a microwaveable bowl and melt, 1 min at a time on about 60% power.

5. Once this has melted add the light brown sugar and mix in. This can be done by hand or with an electric mixer.

6. Add the eggs one at a time until combined. Then either fold in the flour or if using an electric mixer on the slowest speed mix in 1 tbsp at a time.

7. Once it is all combined, pour the brownie mix into the baking tin, reserving a couple of tablespoons of mixture.

8. Pour the cheesecake mix on top and swirl into the brownie. Add the last bit of brownie mix on top and swirl into the cheese mix. Scatter the milk chocolate buttons on top.

9. Place in the oven for 35/45 mins until the cheese mix is set, but it still has a slight wobble in the middle.

10. Leave to cool in the tin and then turn out onto a wire rack. Cut when cold.

Should be kept refrigerated, but is best eaten at room temperature.

Extras:
I rarely make a plain brownie, as I like to add extra flavours. Here are a couple of ideas to have a go at.
Add 150g raspberries-scatter half on top of the brownie mix and the rest on top of the cheese mix.
Add 100g hazelnuts-mix half into the brownie and scatter the rest on top of the cheese.
Add 2 tbsp chopped mint-mix the mint into the brownie mix. Once the brownie has cooked and cooled slightly add mint balls to the top of the brownie.
Once you've got the hang of it, why not experiment with your own flavours.
You can easily substitute the plain flour for gluten free flour with the same results.

EL KANTINA

El Kantina is a fully mobile street food catering company serving fresh, tasty and feisty Mexican and Southern street food...with a twist. It's twisted Tex-Mex!

We combine our love of good food with our top secret recipes to create an array of succulent dishes including our 'Cowboy Burrito', 'Baby Doll Taco' or 'Chow Down Chorizo Chilli Nachos'. All our tasty meals are freshly prepared and use only the best ethically sourced Yorkshire ingredients.

Inspired by traditional, authentic recipes which are then given the El Kantina 'pimp-up', you'll find our tasty tex-mex at festivals, events and weddings across the country!
www.elkantina.co.uk

NINJA NACHOS

Takes 6 hours to cook /20 mins preparation time
Serves 6 people

You'll need
For the Pulled Pork:
2 tbsp spice mix
2kg pork shoulder
4 large onions
4 mixed peppers
1 garlic head

For the Nachos:
150g butter
1 pint of milk
200g cheese
chilli sauce, to taste
salt and pepper
large bag of tortilla chips

For the Salsa:
6 large tomatoes
2 onions
1 tbsp jalapeños
1 handful of coriander
salt and pepper
1 tsp sugar
1 tbsp white wine vinegar

Mexican & Southern Street Food

RECIPE

How to do it:

1. Rub approx. 2kg Yorkshire Pork Shoulder with a spice mix - we use our own Mexican spice blend (secret recipe!) You could try dried cumin, paprika, garlic salt, coriander or whatever you fancy.

2. Leave in the fridge for as long as you can, so that all of the flavour seeps into the meat.

3. Fry off onions, peppers, tomatoes and garlic in a large saucepan until softened. Add the meat to the pan and place in a pre-heated oven on a low setting for 6 hours. Once cooked, the meat should 'pull' apart and is ready to eat.

4. For extra juicy Pulled Pork, add BBQ sauce to the meat (we make our own but you can buy good quality versions from the shops!)

To Prepare the Nachos
Chilli Cheese Sauce:
Make a roux from butter and flour and add milk gradually to make a thick but runny sauce. Add cheese, salt and pepper and your favourite chilli sauce (we use our own Louisiana Hot Sauce) to make a yummy chilli cheese sauce.

Salsa:
Chop some de-seeded tomatoes, onions, jalapenos, coriander and a little chopped garlic and mix together.

Add some sugar, salt and pepper and leave to sit in the fridge until ready to eat (the flavour will improve over time).

Fill a bowl with your favourite tortilla chips, add a layer of pulled meat and top with the runny cheese sauce, salsa and a few extra Jalapenos if desired! We like to add a blob of sour cream and some chopped red onion to make it extra special.

STREET FOOD

TASTY EXTRAS

'Us Yorkshire folk' are notoriously proud of our culinary offerings, with our great county playing host to the largest concentration of food and drink establishments in the UK. While most of these have already been collected and bundled up into bite size portions just for your pleasure, there are always some fine eateries which don't quite fit into our categories! So, here follows a list of those quirky and wonderful oddities which grace Yorkshire, and while they may not fit into an eatery stereotype by definition, they most certainly do in terms of the quality of food and drink provided.

MY ORGANIC HOME

We are a small home-baking business based in the pretty village of Haworth. Having always used local and organic produce at home, in September 2014 we decided to extend it into the business and re-brand as My Organic Home. All of our delicious cakes are freshly made using the finest organic and local ingredients where possible.

hello@myorganichome.co.uk
www.myorganichome.co.uk

ORGANIC TRIPLE TOFFEE CAKE

You'll need

For the Cake:
350g organic unsalted butter
350g unrefined light muscovado sugar
6 organic medium eggs
2 tsp organic vanilla extract
350g organic self-raising flour

For the Topping:
100g organic toffees
70ml organic double cream

For the Buttercream:
120g organic unsalted butter
30g unrefined light muscovado sugar
1 tbsp organic golden syrup
½ tbsp organic double cream
½ tsp organic vanilla extract
100g organic icing sugar

How to do it:

1. Pre-heat the oven to gas mark 3. Grease and line two 20cm cake tins.
2. Beat the butter and sugar together until light and fluffy.
3. Beat in the eggs, vanilla and flour. Mix until you have a smooth batter.
4. Divide between the two cake tins and level the tops with the back of a spoon.
5. Bake for 35-40 minutes or until risen and spring back when touched. Keep an eye on them after 35 minutes as every oven performs differently.
6. Whilst the cake is baking make the toffee buttercream.
7. Place 40g of the butter in a pan with the light muscovado sugar and the Golden Syrup. Heat on low until it's a deep amber colour.
8. Remove from the heat, add the cream and vanilla extract whilst stirring. Leave to cool.
9. Beat the remaining butter (80g) until smooth, add the icing sugar and beat until pale.
10. Add in the cooled toffee mixture and fully incorporate the two. Leave aside whilst you make the topping.
11. Heat 80g of the toffees with the cream, stirring continuously until melted and combined.
12. Cool until thick, but stir regularly to avoid the top crystalising.
13. Now you can assemble the cake. Take one of the cakes and slice off the raised top so that both the bottom and top of the cake are flat. Place it on a cake board and then spread the buttercream all over it, using a palette knife.
14. Now place the second cake on top ensuring the bottom of the sponge sits on the buttercream.
If you prefer you can cut both sponges in half to create more layers
15. Now spoon the thickened and cooled toffee sauce over the top of the cake.
16. For the finishing touch, take the remaining toffees and chop them up using either a sharp knife or Kitchen Chopper. Sprinkle these on top of the cake.

TIP - If you are using a cake board, spread a small bit of buttercream on it before you place the first sponge to act like a bit of glue!

YORKSHIRE PUDD

Christopher Blackburn is the world's reigning Yorkshire Pudding Champion. He made his TV debut on ITV's Food Glorious Food and has gone on to appear in many other television programmes, from Countryfile to The One Show. Chris has demonstrated to Mary Berry his technique for world-class Yorkshire Puddings, and has also given Chris Evans and Matt Baker a crash course in his home county's delicacy.

He now runs the award-winning Yorkshire Pudd blog, which focuses on regional food, drink and restaurants.

www.YorkshirePudd.co.uk

ROAST BEEF, YORKSHIRE PUDDING & GRAVY

For the Rib of Beef, you'll need:
1 tbsp mustard powder
1 tbsp plain flour
1 onion, cut in half
salt and black pepper

For the Gravy, you'll need:
1 litre beef stock
2 sprigs of thyme
3 red onions
4 large chopped tomatoes (fresh)
375ml red wine

For the Yorkshire Puddings, you'll need:
225g sieved plain flour
4 eggs
300ml semi-skimmed milk
½ tsp white pepper
1 tsp salt
12 pea-sized pieces of beef dripping

How to do it, for the beef:
1. Mix together the flour and mustard powder, then rub into the fat of the beef.

2. Season with salt and pepper.

3. Sit the beef in a roasting tin together with the onion and season with salt and pepper.

4. To cook the beef a perfect medium rare, roast for 55 mins per kg plus 20 mins at 180°C.

For the gravy:
1. Discard any excess fat left in the roasting tin (this could be used for the Yorkshire Puddings), then place the roasting tin over a medium heat and add the sprigs of thyme, onions and tomatoes.

2. Cook for 5-6 mins, add the wine, then bring the liquid to a simmer and use a potato masher to extract all the flavour from the tomatoes (this will help thicken the gravy).

3. Increase the heat and add the stock, allowing it to bubble for about 10 mins until reduced by half.

4. Pass the gravy through a sieve, bring back to the boil and reduce to a gravy consistency.

For the Yorkshire Puddings:
1. Sift flour and salt into a large bowl, add the beaten eggs and half the milk, then whisk until it resembles wallpaper paste (it needs to be very smooth).

2. Add the rest of the milk and again whisk to form the batter, then let it rest for 30 mins (this can be speeded up by placing it in the fridge for 10 mins).

3. Put a muffin tray, with ½ tsp of beef dripping in each hole, in the oven at the highest possible temperature (normally 270°C) until your hear the oven click and reach temperature.

4. Remove the muffin tray and pour in the batter (about ½ to ¾ way up each hole), then place back in the oven and reduce the temperature immediately to 200°C (bake for 25 mins).

CURRY CUISINE COOKERY SCHOOL

Whenever I want to conjure up a taste of home, it's a mix of flavours from my native Bradford, my Gujarati Kenyan mother and Indian father.

My cooking has elements of many different worlds and my background has given me a huge amount of inspiration. My mother was always busy in the kitchen and my siblings and I mucked in. My spicing has a definite Gujarati Kenyan slant, with a little of my father's flavour thrown in and some Ugandan from my mother-in-law.

In 2007, I left a career as an accountant to set up a cookery school from my home in Wakefield and then, with my husband Paresh, developed a range of chutneys and spice mixes.

Our school is informal and family orientated. For me, it's always been about communicating what I know and sharing my culture and food with others. Gujarat cuisine is less well known in the UK and I've been able to pass on these traditions and flavours to other families.

Prett Tejura
(founder)

www.currycuisinecookeryschool.co.uk

CHICKEN MASALA

You'll need:
600g chicken breasts, chopped into small squares
1 medium onion, finely chopped
5cm stick cinnamon
4 cloves
2 tbsp sunflower oil
1½ tsp crushed garlic
1 tsp chopped ginger
200g chopped tomatoes
1 tsp salt (to your taste)
2 tsp coriander and cumin powder
1 tsp garam masala
½ tsp turmeric powder
¼ tsp red chilli powder
1 tsp chopped green chillies
handful fresh coriander chopped

How to do it:

1. Place the oil in a cooking pan and heat, then add cloves and cinnamon and wait until they sizzle.

2. Add the onions and cook, on a medium to low heat, stirring occasionally until they turn golden (they may take up to 10 minutes).

3. Add the garlic and ginger, sauté for 1 minute to release any raw aromas, then add the powdered spices and salt, cooking for 1 minute while stirring.

4. Add a little water if the paste begins to stick, then add the tomatoes and green chillies.

5. Simmer for 5-10 minutes with the lid on (the masala will be ready when oil appears on the surface).

6. Place the chicken in the pan and stir until the masala is well mixed into the meat, then cook on high heat (with lid on) for approx. 5 minutes to sear the chicken.

7. Reduce the heat to low and cook for a further 15-20 minutes, stirring occasionally (pour approx. 50ml hot water into the pan if required).

8. Add the fresh coriander, cook for a further 5 minutes, then serve with boiled basmati rice or chapattis.

(Serves 4)

SHEPHERDS PURSE ARTISAN CHEESES

Shepherds Purse Cheeses began in the 1980s after farmer's wife, Judy Bell, discovered her passion and talent for cheese making. Her mission was to create quality dairy alternatives for those who suffer from cow's milk allergies.

Judy discovered that ewe's milk is a delicious alternative and, for over a year, she researched different breeds of sheep and experimented with a variety of traditional methods of artisan cheese making. She even purchased her own flock of milking sheep to ensure a quality supply.

After another year of running the farm, bringing up a young family and perfecting recipes, Judy was ready. Shepherds Purse, with the first cheeses, Yorkshire Fettle and Olde York, was officially launched at the Great Yorkshire Show in 1989.

Any doubts were swept aside by the warm reception from the public. Shepherds Purse went on to win the first of many awards at the prestigious Nantwich International Cheese Show, with a gold medal for Olde York.

Over 25 years, the artisan cheese company has grown, adding new innovative cheeses using cow's milk and buffalo milk. In 1994, Judy was proud to bring back blue-cheese making to Yorkshire after an absence of 30 years, producing the now famous Yorkshire Blue, Mrs Bell's Blue and a recent addition, Harrogate Blue.

Today, the company is run by Judy's daughters, Katie and Caroline, and makes a range of award-winning cheeses which can be found on the best deli counters and restaurant menus across the globe. Most-recent awards include gold medals at the British Cheese Awards 2014 for Harrogate Blue and Yorkshire Fettle.

www.shepherdspurse.co.uk

HARROGATE BLUE MASH

This is a really simple way to create a hearty luxurious dish. Serve simply with peas, meat and homemade gravy for a full-on winter warmer. (Serves 4)

You'll need:
900g floury potatoes, Desiree or Maris Piper
100g unsalted butter
150g Harrogate Blue cheese
50ml full-fat milk
4 tbsp double cream

How to do it:
1. Peel the potatoes just before cooking and cut into even sized chunks, put them into a pan with cold water and a little salt, then bring to the boil.

2. Reduce the heat and simmer until just tender (test by inserting a sharp knife).

3. Drain well in a colander and return to the pan, then mash them immediately.

4. Warm the milk gently, beat the butter with a wooden spoon, then gradually mix in the warm milk followed by the cream.

5. Add to the mashed potatoes and beat until fluffy and light (the mash should be buttery creamy and velvety in texture).

6. Finally cube or crumble the cheese into 1cm cubes and gently fold into the mash (the golden colour will swirl through the potato as the cheese melts).

7. Garnish with parsley and serve.

VINCENTS

Based in York, a city well known for its wide variety of independent food and drink retailers, Vincent's coffee was founded in order to provide exceptional and ethically sourced coffee. Our 100% Arabica beans come from all across the world and are freshly roasted just outside of the city. We take great care to continually review our supply chains to ensure transparency and accountability.

Vincent's Coffee can be found online and in local retailers, with both whole bean and ground blends on offer.
www.vincentscoffee.com

ESPRESSO HAZELNUT BROWNIES

These brownies are made deliciously decadent with the addition of fresh espresso and hazelnut spread. Use a South American coffee for a full bodied mocha finish, or alternatively an African coffee will give you notes of fruit and citrus.

Makes approximately - 16 thick slices
Preparation time - 15 minutes plus 55 minutes cooking time.
You'll need:
30 x 32cm tray bake or roasting tin
300g plain chocolate, use dark chocolate for an even richer flavour
225g unsalted butter
double espresso made from double espresso made from Arabica beans
3 large eggs
175g caster sugar
100g self-raising flour
2 tbsp hazelnut spread

How to do it:
1. Pre heat the oven to 190°C (gas mark 5) and line your tin with greaseproof paper.

2. Break the chocolate up into pieces and slowly melt in a bowl with the butter over a pan of hot water, stirring as you go. Once the chocolate pieces have completely melted, add the hazelnut spread and stir until combined. Take the mixture off the heat to cool.

3. In another bowl, beat the sugar, eggs and double espresso together. Slowly add this into your cooled chocolate mixture, then gently fold in the self-raising flour.

4. Bake in the oven for 55 minutes, the brownies will crack on the surface and remain gooey in the centre. Leave the brownies to cool for half an hour in the tin before finally cutting them into 16 pieces.

BUSY BEES

Busy Bees Nursery in Guiseley provides quality childcare for under 5s, in a fantastic purpose built environment, dedicated to ensuring that every child's needs are met.

However, it isn't just the childcare that this place offers, as not only do the children receive top quality care, they also receive delicious food!

The nursery is proud to have been awarded the Silver Award for Life from the Soil Association in recognition of their commitment to using quality ingredients in every meal and snack prepared on site. Busy Bees provides children with fresh, nutritious and well-balanced meals every day, which ensures that they receive all of the nutrients needed to help them flourish.

www.busybeeschildcare.co.uk/nursery/guiseley

BIENENSTICH (BEE STING CAKE)

The Bienenstich is a delicious dessert often eaten at family gatherings. It is a traditional German cake made from a yeast dough, topped with caramelised almonds and filled with a whipped cream and custard mix.

You'll need

For the Dough Mix:
250g plain flour   ½ pinch of salt
½ cube fresh yeast   1 egg
50g caster sugar   125ml milk (lukewarm)
1 tsp vanilla essence or   500g butter (cubed)
flavouring

For the topping:
75g butter
50g caster sugar
1 tsp vanilla essence/flavouring
1 tbsp honey
2 tbsp cream
75g flaked almonds

For the filling:
5 leaves of gelatine
1 packet of instant custard (of course a 'real' custard can be made, however, for ease an instant custard powder can be used instead)
250ml milk
400ml whipping cream

How to do it:

1. Sift the flour into a bowl making a mould in the middle and flaking the yeast into it. Add a small amount of the sugar and all of the lukewarm milk and leave to dissolve and froth for 10 minutes.

2. Add the rest of the sugar, vanilla essence, salt, egg and butter and knead to form a smooth dough. Cover the mixing bowl with a tea towel and leave the dough to prove for 40 minutes.

3. Meanwhile, prepare the topping by melting the butter, sugar, vanilla essence, honey and cream until simmering. Turn off the heat and stir in the flaked almonds. Set aside to cool.

4. Soak the gelatine in cold water for 5 minutes. Cook the custard using the instant power and milk until thickened and stir in the gelatine leaves one by one after squeezing out excess water. Leave the custard to cool completely. Whip the cream until stiff and fold in the cooled custard.

5. Briefly knead the dough and roll it out to fit into either a 26cm springform or a 20x30cm rectangular baking tray. Spread the topping evenly onto the rolled out dough and leave to rise again for about 15 minutes. Preheat the oven to 175°C (fan oven), 190°C (conventional oven). Bake the cake for about 20 minutes or until well risen and golden brown on top. Take the cake out of the oven and leave to cool completely.

6. Once cooled cut the cake horizontally, so you have two halves. Spread the filling evenly onto the bottom layer and place the top layer back onto the filling. Cut the cake and enjoy.

BOXPIZZA

Boxpizza was established in 2007 and is now recognised as the leading independent pizza takeaway in Leeds. Boxpizza offers its customers a takeaway pizza experience with a difference.

With locally sourced toppings (all fresh meat is 100% Yorkshire sourced!) all prepared in house, along with a delicious traditional sourdough pizza dough recipe, Boxpizza aims to provide a restaurant quality pizza delivered straight to your door!

Choose from a vast range of pizzas, including meaty, spicy and veggie (some with a particularly Yorkshire based influence), however, if that doesn't quite do it for you, Boxpizza also provides traditional piadanas. A speciality of the Romagna region of Italy, piadana is a freshly grilled flatbread filled with the freshest and most delicious toppings!

Unit 3, The Triangle, 2 Burley Road, Leeds, LS3 1JB
Tel: 0113 2445544
www.boxpizza.co.uk

GRILLED CHICKEN FLORENTINE PIZZA

This pizza was on our menu as a chef's special for a while and proved very popular. Here is the recipe for you to re-create at home.

Makes two 11" pizzas. Takes approximately half an hour to make the dough plus 4 hours proving time. Approximately 15 minutes to then roll and add the toppings. Baking time around 15 minutes.

You'll need

For the Pizza Dough:
250g pizza flour
or strong white bread flour
135g room temperature water
5g sea salt
5g sugar
8g dried active yeast (or 5g fresh yeast)
10g extra virgin olive oil

For the Tomato Sauce:
1 tin of good quality chopped tomatoes
pinch of salt
pinch of black pepper
1 tbsp dried oregano

For the Pizza Toppings:
150g grated mozzarella cheese (you could also use sliced baby mozzarella if preferred)
1 fresh chicken breast with skin removed
1 tin of canned spinach
100g sun dried tomatoes
1 sliced red onion
parmesan cheese to grate

How to do it:
1. First make the pizza dough. This can be done with a food mixer with a dough hook or can be kneaded by hand. A food mixer will give better results if available.

2. Tip the flour, salt, sugar and yeast into the mixing bowl. If using a mixer to make the dough, start the mixer off on low speed. Slowly add the water until all the flour is incorporated into the water. Once a dough has formed, turn the mixer to the fastest setting and mix for around 5 minutes.

3. Add the olive oil and mix on fast speed for 1 minute only until the oil has been absorbed. The dough should now be smooth and feel springy.

N.B. If making by hand, repeat the steps above but knead by hand for around 15-20 minutes until the dough feels springy and smooth, adding the oil towards the end of kneading.

4. Once the dough has been made, weigh in to 2 separate balls approximately 205g in weight each.Then form the dough by rolling in the palm of your hand on the work surface into a smooth ball.

5. Put the 2 balls onto some greaseproof paper and cover with a damp towel. Allow to rise for around 3-4 hours until roughly doubled in size.

While the dough is proving, prepare the grilled chicken and tomato sauce.

For the Grilled Chicken:
1. Heat a large griddle or frying pan. At the same time pre-heat the oven to around 150°C. Season the chicken breast with salt and pepper and coat with vegetable oil.

2. Grill the chicken until dark golden brown on both sides before transferring to the warm oven to cook through. Ensure the chicken is cooked through before slicing into strips.

For the Tomato Sauce:
1. Simply blend the tomatoes, salt, pepper and oregano in a food processor or hand blender.

Once the dough is ready, it's time to assemble the pizza!
Heat a pizza stone or baking tray in the oven on the highest temperature possible.

1. On your work surface, throw down some flour and roll out the pizza dough by hand or with a rolling pin until you have achieved a round(ish) flat piece of dough around 10-11" wide.

2. Add the tomato sauce and spread around the base, leaving enough for a nice crust around the edge. Remove the hot pizza stone or baking tray from the oven and slide the pizza base and tomato sauce onto the tray.

3. Put it back in the oven for around 30 seconds to a minute to slightly cook the dough. Then remove the baking tray or pizza stone along with the pizza base and place on a heat resistant surface (a wooden chopping board is ideal).

4. For the toppings, add the mozzarella cheese to the partly cooked pizza base and spread out. Top with the sliced grilled chicken, sliced red onion, spinach and sun dried tomatoes.

5. Put the now fully assembled pizza back in the oven and bake for around 10-15 minutes until the dough and cheese are nicely browned.

6. Remove from the oven and top with grated Parmesan cheese. Cut the pizza into slices and serve with a large glass of your favourite wine!

THE TEAM

THE TASTY TEAM

We are the Hallmark Million Makers! We are Joel, Jackie, Lois, Katie C,
Beth, Katie W & Zully. When deciding how we were going to raise our
money, the idea for the book was a no brainer - each of us working and
living in Yorkshire, and all of us passionate about food (some of us
more so about the eating than the cooking!) - we therefore wanted to
share our favourite recipes with you. We really hope you enjoy them!

We would also like to take this opportunity to say a massive THANK YOU
to all of you who bought this book, helping us raise lots of money for
such an amazing cause. You have all helped The Prince's Trust continue
to make a difference in young peoples' lives across the UK.

All net proceeds donated to The Prince's Trust (registered charity no. 1079675)

JOEL
CUMIN LAMB CHOPS WITH SPICY MOROCCAN RICE

You'll need:
100g basmati rice
½ stock cube
6 lamb chops
1 tbsp olive oil
1 onion, chopped
1 garlic clove, chopped
1 tbsp pine nuts
1 tsp each ground cumin and coriander
4 dried apricots, chopped
chopped coriander
1 lemon, cut into wedges

How to do it:
1. Put the rice in a pan, cover with water and add the stock cube. Bring to the boil and then simmer for 10-12 mins until the rice is tender.
2. Heat the grill and season the chops with salt, pepper and cumin. Grill for 3-4 mins on each side until cooked to your liking.
3. Chop the onions, garlic, apricots and coriander.
4. Heat the oil in a pan, add the onion and fry gently for 5 mins until lightly coloured.
5. Add the garlic and pine nuts then fry until the nuts are lightly roasted. Stir in ground cumin, add the apricots and rice and stir well, heating everything through.
6. Add the coriander to the rice mix, stir well and serve with the chops. Add the lemon wedges so they can be squeezed over.

JACKIE

MUSHROOM RISOTTO

You'll need:
1 pack of mushrooms (large or small your choice)
1 onion
1 garlic clove
1 large glass of white wine
black pepper
100g arborio risotto rice
1 pack bacon lardons (I prefer smoked)
2 pints of beef stock (you could use chicken or vegetable stock)
1oz of butter
4 tablespoons parmesan cheese

How to do it:
1. Slice onion finely and wash and slice the mushrooms.
2. In a frying pan or wok cook the bacon lardons.
3. In another pan (or saucepan) add half a cup of water, mushrooms, crushed garlic and black pepper. Cover, heat and simmer until cooked.
4. When the lardons have browned and crisped remove from the pan to a side plate leaving the fat in the pan. Add the onions to the pan and cook until softened and brown. Add the lardons back to the onion and mix together for a couple of minutes.
5. Add the risotto rice and stir through until the fat has been absorbed from the pan.
6. Add the wine to the mixture and half of the stock. Bring this to boil (approx. 2-3mins)
7. When boiled turn down heat, cover pan and leave to simmer checking every couple of minutes that there is still liquid (approx. 10mins).
8. Add the remaining stock as required until the rice has softened.
9. Add the mushrooms (and liquid) and stir in.
10. When the rice has softened and most of the liquid has evaporated add the butter and parmesan cheese and fold in. Turn off the heat and cover for 2 minutes. Then serve and enjoy!

BETH
MUSHROOM AND SALMON TAGLIATELLE

You'll need:
2 salmon fillets
200g dried tagliatelle pasta
200g chestnut mushrooms, sliced
1 small leek, trimmed and cut into 5mm slices
handful frozen peas
4 tbsp half-fat crème fraiche
2 tbsp grated parmesan cheese (optional)
1 tsp extra virgin olive oil
flaked sea salt
freshly ground black pepper

How to do it:
1. Preheat your oven to 200°C/Fan 180°C/Gas 6. Take a sheet of foil roughly 30cm x 30cm/12in x 12in and place the salmon fillets, skin-side down, in the centre of the foil.
2. Season with salt and pepper. Bring the sides of the foil up and crimp together to create a sealed parcel. Place on a baking tray in the oven to cook for 10-15 minutes, or until the salmon is cooked through (the flesh should be opaque and flake easily).
3. Half fill a large saucepan with boiling water. Add the pasta and cook for 10-12 minutes or until tender, stirring occasionally.
4. Whilst the pasta is cooking put 1tsp oil in a medium non-stick frying pan and fry the leeks and mushrooms together for 8-10 minutes, stirring occasionally.
Add the frozen peas to the pasta 2 minutes before the pasta is ready. 5. Drain the pasta and peas in a colander, then put back into the saucepan. Add the mushrooms and leeks. Spoon over the crème fraiche and add the cheese (optional).
6. Season with a good pinch of salt and lots of ground black pepper. Lighty toss together. Divide the pasta equally between two bowls and place cooked salmon on top.

LOIS
CHICKEN SATAY

You'll need:
1 tbsp medium curry powder
thumb-size piece of ginger
2 garlic cloves
zest and juice of 2 limes
1 fresh chilli
2 tbsp soy sauce
6 tbsp crunchy peanut butter (or smooth peanut butter)
10 skinless boneless thighs
handful of fresh coriander

How to do it:
1. In a blender, blitz the garlic, half a chilli, ginger, curry powder, lime juice and zest of limes, soy sauce and peanut butter into a paste and add a bit of cold water to loosen the sauce. Season if needed.
2. Cut the chicken up ready to skewer.
3. Marinate the chicken with 2/3 thirds of the marinade and leave the rest for a dip. Thread the chicken through the skewers and marinade for a few hours or even better overnight.
4. Heat up the frying pan with a tablespoon of oil and then fry the skewers, alternating regularly for 15 minutes or until cooked.
5. Serve with a sprinkling of coriander and chilli plus the rest of the satay sauce. Enjoy!

Sycamore chopping board hand crafted by local designer
Felix Taylor (felixtaylordesigns@gmail.com)

KATIE W

THAI GREEN CURRY NOODLES

You'll need:
vegetable oil
2 boneless chicken breasts
1 large courgette
½ bunch of spring onions
2 cloves of garlic
thumb sized piece of ginger
2 tbsp green curry paste
250ml chicken stock
½ tin coconut milk
1 tbsp fish sauce
100g salted peanuts
100g medium egg noodles
1 lime

How to do it:
1. Add a splash: of the oil to a hot wok. Dice the chicken, and add to the wok. Stir fry until golden brown. Remove and set aside.
2. Add another splash of oil if the wok has dried up. Dice the courgette and add to the wok until golden brown.
3. Chop the spring onion, garlic and ginger and add them to the wok. Stir fry for another minute, and then add the curry paste and give it a good stir so everything is coated in the paste.
4. Pour in the chicken stock, coconut and fish sauce. Bring to the boil and simmer for about 15 mins to allow the flavours to develop.
5. Add the peanuts and the reserved chicken, and cook for a further 5mins or until the sauce has thickened & reduced a little.
6. Meanwhile, cook the noodles in a separate pan according to the pack instructions. Once they are ready and the sauce has thickened to a good consistency, stir the noodles into the sauce.
7. Alternatively, you can serve the sauce with some basmati rice. However, once I discovered noodles with this dish, I never looked back! Serve with lime wedges.

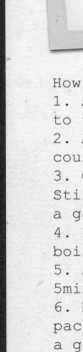

ZULLY

SAMOSA

You'll need:

1 whole garlic crushed
2lb mixed keema
bag of mixed frozen vegetables
10 potatoes- diced
3 finely chopped onions
10 green chillies finely chopped
1 tin of chopped tomatoes
fist full of jeera and garam masala
vegetable oil
5 tbsp of salt (to own taste)
handful of green coriander

1 large bag of plain flour
1 tbsp salt
1 glass of oil
1/2 glass of melted butter

How to do it:

1. Brown the garlic in 3 table spoons of oil, throw in the keema and stir on high for 5 minutes.
2. Add onions, chillies, salt, jeera, tomatoes and mixed vegetables.
3. Put on medium heat for two hours stirring occasionally (make sure keema doesn't start sticking). Then add garam masala and potatoes Once potatoes soften, add coriander and turn off the heat.
4. For the pastry, you need one large bag of plain flour, a tablespoon of salt, one glass of oil and half a glass of melted butter. You need to put all ingredients into a bowl and add water gradually while kneading until dough is soft and smooth.
5. Divide the dough into approximately 30 small balls. Shape each ball into a flat 1cm thick circle.
6. Put onto a warm flat griddle (chapatti) pan (3 secs on each side).
7. Take the cooked dough and slice through the middle. Take one half and glue (a paste made with self-raising flour and water) one half of the edge to make a pocket.
8. Add the Keema and close with some more glue into a triangle shape making sure there are no holes
9. Freeze for at least 1 hour before frying till golden brown (deep pan vegetable oil).

KATIE C

CARAMELISED ONION, AUBERGINE & GOATS CHEESE TARTS

You'll need:
150g soft goat's cheese
fresh thyme to garnish
clear honey to drizzle once cooked
3 red onions, finely sliced
1 tbsp light brown sugar
1 tbsp balsamic vinegar
1 aubergine, sliced into 1 cm thick slices
375g pack of pre-rolled puff pastry
olive oil for cooking

How to do it:
1. Heat one tablespoon of olive oil in a pan, add the red onions, cover and cook for 10 mins over a medium heat, stir occasionally.
2. Remove the lid and add the sugar and balsamic vinegar and cook for a further 5 minutes on a high heat until the onions have caramelised.
3. Brush the aubergine slices with olive oil and griddle or fry until tender (roughly 3-4 minutes on each side).
4. Roll out the pastry and cut out disks using a glass (roughly 8-9 cm in diameter) you should get approx. 10-12 tarts out of one roll of pastry. Put the disks onto a lined baking tray and divide the onion mixture between the tarts leaving 1 cm border around the edge.
5. Next, top with the aubergine slices. Pile these up and then top with the goat's cheese.
6. Preheat the oven to 200°C. Bake the tarts for 25 minutes until the pastry is puffed and golden, cover the tarts with foil for the final 10 minutes.
7. Once out of the oven, drizzle with honey and top with thyme. The tarts can be enjoyed hot or cold and are perfect as appetisers or for a lunchtime treat!

THANK YOU

TO ALL OUR LOVELY SPONSORS!

A massive thanks to all our sponsors, without them this book wouldn't have been printed for you to enjoy!

CARDINAL

RETAIL & COMMERCIAL INTERIORS

ViSION

In Yorkshire we call a spade a spade...

JACKSON'S
Yorkshire's
CHAMPION BREAD

And what's our bread?
That's always "Champion"

BLACKS
SOLICITORS

WALKER FOSTER
wf
SOLICITORS

™

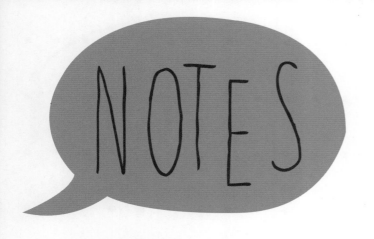